CAMBRIDGE LIBRARY COLLECTION
Books of enduring scholarly value

Travel, Europe

This collection of narratives contains vivid accounts of the varied landscapes, built environment and customs encountered by eighteenth- and nineteenth-century travellers in the British Isles and Europe. Some were wealthy individuals on the Grand Tour, while others were travelling on business, for pleasure, in pursuit of better health, or simply to escape trouble at home.

A Tour in Switzerland

The radical writer and poet Helen Maria Williams (1759–1827) is best remembered for her eight-volume *Letters from France* (1790–6), charting the progress of the French Revolution. Having published poetry and a novel, *Julia* (1790), she travelled to France, where her salon welcomed the likes of Mary Wollstonecraft, Thomas Paine and leading Girondists. Forced to flee the country in 1794, she went into exile in Switzerland for six months, travelling with the printer and political reformer John Hurford Stone (1763–1818). This two-volume account of the journeys she made during her time there, first published in 1798, documents what she sees as the failure of Swiss democracy. Highlighting the shortcomings of the Swiss government and the suffering of much of Swiss society through exploitation, Williams anticipates revolutionary activity in the cantons. Volume 1 concentrates primarily on Basel and its canton.

Cambridge University Press has long been a pioneer in the reissuing of out-of-print titles from its own backlist, producing digital reprints of books that are still sought after by scholars and students but could not be reprinted economically using traditional technology. The Cambridge Library Collection extends this activity to a wider range of books which are still of importance to researchers and professionals, either for the source material they contain, or as landmarks in the history of their academic discipline.

Drawing from the world-renowned collections in the Cambridge University Library and other partner libraries, and guided by the advice of experts in each subject area, Cambridge University Press is using state-of-the-art scanning machines in its own Printing House to capture the content of each book selected for inclusion. The files are processed to give a consistently clear, crisp image, and the books finished to the high quality standard for which the Press is recognised around the world. The latest print-on-demand technology ensures that the books will remain available indefinitely, and that orders for single or multiple copies can quickly be supplied.

The Cambridge Library Collection brings back to life books of enduring scholarly value (including out-of-copyright works originally issued by other publishers) across a wide range of disciplines in the humanities and social sciences and in science and technology.

A Tour in Switzerland

Or, a View of the Present State of the Governments and Manners of those Cantons: With Comparative Sketches of the Present State of Paris

Volume 1

Helen Maria Williams

CAMBRIDGE
UNIVERSITY PRESS

University Printing House, Cambridge, CB2 8BS, United Kingdom

Published in the United States of America by Cambridge University Press, New York

Cambridge University Press is part of the University of Cambridge.

It furthers the University's mission by disseminating knowledge in the pursuit of education, learning and research at the highest international levels of excellence.

www.cambridge.org
Information on this title: www.cambridge.org/9781108065948

© in this compilation Cambridge University Press 2013

This edition first published 1798
This digitally printed version 2013

ISBN 978-1-108-06594-8 Paperback

This book reproduces the text of the original edition. The content and language reflect the beliefs, practices and terminology of their time, and have not been updated.

Cambridge University Press wishes to make clear that the book, unless originally published by Cambridge, is not being republished by, in association or collaboration with, or with the endorsement or approval of, the original publisher or its successors in title.

A TOUR

IN

SWITZERLAND;

OR,

A VIEW OF THE PRESENT STATE, &c.

A TOUR

SWITZERLAND;

OR,

A VIEW OF THE PRESENT STATE

OF THE

GOVERNMENTS AND MANNERS

OF THOSE

CANTONS:

WITH COMPARATIVE SKETCHES

OF

THE PRESENT STATE OF PARIS.

By *HELEN MARIA WILLIAMS*.

VOL. I.

LONDON:
PRINTED FOR G. G. AND J. ROBINSON, PATERNOSTER-ROW.

M,DCC,XCVIII.

PREFACE.

IN prefenting to the Public a View of Switzerland, a country of which fo much has been already written, it may perhaps become me to clear myfelf from the charge of prefumption. The defcriptive parts of this journal were rapidly traced with the ardor of a fond imagination, eager to feize the vivid colouring of the moment ere it fled, and give permanence to the emotions of admiration, while the folemn enthufiafm beat high in my bofom; but when the fenfations excited by thofe views of majeftic grandeur had fubfided, I recollected, with regret, that the paths which I had delighted

PREFACE.

to tread had been trodden before; and that the objects on which I had gazed with aftonifhment had been already defcribed. It is true, that the fketch I have penciled of that fublime fcenery, however rude, will be found to be an original drawing, copied from nature, and not from books; yet I fhould fcarcely have prefumed to obtrude that unfinifhed outline on the public eye, if the other parts of my journal offered nothing new to its obfervation. It is the prefent moral fituation of Switzerland that juftifies the appearance of thefe volumes, in which an attempt is made to trace the important effects which the French Revolution has produced in that country, and which are about to unfold a new æra in its hiftory. The governments of Switzerland, placed within reach of the electrical fire of that Revolution, flafhing around all their borders, behold the fubtle fpark, which finds a conductor in the human heart, efcaping beyond

PREFACE.

yond its prescribed limits, and feel its strong concussion in every agitated nerve.

I have endeavoured to give an additional interest to my journal, by connecting the view of the manners and customs of the Swiss towns, with a comparative picture of the present state of Paris; and I offer this Work to the Public with far less hope from the experience of its past indulgence, than solicitude to obtain its future favor.

CONTENTS.

CHAP. I.

Introduction.—Motives of my Journey to Switzerland.—Road from Paris to Basil.—Basil.—Reflections on Switzerland.—Dispositions and Occupations of the Inhabitants of Basil.—Manners.—Smoaking Clubs.—Female Societies.—Public Amusements.

CHAP. II.

Comparative View of the Spirit of Commerce in France, before, and since the Revolution.—Paper System.—Female Traders and Contractors.

CHAP. III.

Amusements of Paris.—Balls.—Festivals.—Supper given by a Contractor.—Dress.—Parallel between a Contractor and

CONTENTS.

and a Stock-holder.—New Aristocracy.—Modern Royalists.—Odeon.—Bals à la Victime.—Tivoli.—Elysium.—Bagatelle and other Public Gardens.—Glaciers of Paris.

CHAP. IV.

Road from Basil into the Canton of Soleure.—Swiss Taste in Gardening.—Visit to a Farm-house.—Rural Ceremonies.—Traditionary Story of the Destruction of a Tyrant.—Baden.—Zurich.—Reflections on the View over the Lake to the Alps.—Fall of the Rhine at Lauffen.—Bridge at Schaffhausen.

CHAP. V.

Lavater.—Fall of Infidelity, and Triumph of the Religion of our Fathers.—Fashionable Devotees.—La Harpe.—Lectures on Religion at Idalia.—Desertion of the Proselytes.—Theophilanthropism.

CHAP. VI.

Country from Basil to Zuric.—Bremgarton.—Balstal.—Ornamented Graves.—French Burials.—Solemnity of Sunday in Switzerland.—Observations on Cruelty to Animals at Paris.—Geographical Religion of Switzerland.

CHAP.

CONTENTS.

CHAP. VII.

Canton of Basil.—Rights of the Burghers of Basil.—Degraded State of the other Classes. — Peasants.—Serfs.—Comparative View of French and Swiss Peasantry before the Revolution.—State of French Peasantry since the Revolution.—Manufactures in the Canton of Basil.—Singular Restrictions on the Laborious Classes.—Jews.—Citizens in France.—Toleration.—Defence of the Jews by a French Catholic Bishop.—Religious Toleration in Turkey.—Whimsical Persecution of the Jews at Basil.—Reflections and Apostrophe of a Jew.

CHAP. VIII.

Government of the Canton of Basil.—Mode of Election of the Members of the Council, and of the Professors of the University.—Ancient and Modern State of Literature.

CHAP. IX.

Curiosities of Basil.—Arsenal.—Cathedral.—Public Library.—Dance of Death.—Departure from Basil.—Sempack.—Reflections on the Love of Freedom.

CHAP.

CONTENTS.

CHAP. X.

Lucerne.—Voyage down the Lake of Lucerne.—Gersau.—Schweitz.— Brunnen.—Tell's Chapel.—Lake of Uri.

CHAP. XI.

Altorf —William Tell.— Ascent to St. Gothard.— Waſſen.—Valley of Schellinen.—Devil's Bridge.— Vale of Urseren.

CHAP. XII.

Top of St. Gothard.—Airolo.

CHAP. XIII.

Valley of Levantine.—Torrents of the Teſſino.—Harveſt-home.

CHAP. XIV.

Government of the Levantine Valley.

CHAP.

CONTENTS.

CHAP. XV.

Government of the Canton of Uri.—Origin of Swiss Freedom.

CHAP. XVI.

Giornico.—Bellinzone.—Mount Cenave.—Lugano.—Lake of Lugano.

CHAP. XVII.

Installation of the Bailiff of Lugano.—Italian Odes.—Sail down the Lake.—Locarno.

CHAP. XVIII.

A Storm on the Lake.—Return to Bellinzone.—Visit to a Convent.—Installation of the Bailiff of Bellinzone.

CHAP. XIX.

History of an Emigrant Family.

CHAP. XX.

Visit to the Grisons.—Discussion on the Revolution.

CHAP.

CONTENTS.

CHAP. XXI.

Val Calenca State of Society.—Journey up St. Bernardin.—Lavanges.—Grison Hospitality.—Pastoral Occupations.

CHAP. XXII.

St. Bernardin.—Misery of the Shepherd's Life.—Emigrant Priest.—Summit of St. Bernardin.—First View of the Rhine.

A TOUR
IN
SWITZERLAND;
OR,
A VIEW OF THE PRESENT STATE, &c.

CHAP. I.

Introduction.—Motives of my Journey to Switzerland.—Road from Paris to Basil.—Basil.—Reflections on Switzerland.—Dispositions and Occupations of the Inhabitants of Basil.—Manners.—Smoaking Clubs.—Female Societies.—Public Amusements.

DURING the period of that new species of tyranny which assumed the name of revolutionary government, I was not merely involved in the common danger which threatened every individual in France, but had claims to particular proscription. It was not only remembered by many of the satellites of Robespierre, that I had been the friend of the Gironde,

Gironde, of Madame Roland, martyred names which it was death to pronounce, but that I had written a work, publifhed in England, in which I had traced, without referve, the characters of our oppreffors; whofe ferocious purpofes I had often heard developed with the glowing eloquence of Vergniaud, and the indignant energy of La Source. No danger could be more imminent than that of living under the very tyranny which I had the perilous honour of having been one of the firft to deprecate, and to proclaim.

In this fituation an opportunity prefented itfelf of obtaining a paffport for Switzerland—A paffport!—they who can judge of all the bleffednefs that word unfolds, are not thofe who, at a fafe diftance from the government of Robefpierre, have heard of its terrific influence, but thofe who were placed within its favage grafp. Alas! at the moment

ment of my escape, how many, immured in the dungeons of the tyrant, vainly wished to purchase, at the price of all they possessed, the privilege of forsaking a country, composed only of executioners and of victims!

The road from Paris to Basil leads for the most part along a level country, which displays a picture of fertility, but few scenes of beauty or grandeur, except a branch of the Vosges, which we traversed near Belfort, and whose swelling mountains, presenting faint traces of those we were going to contemplate, we saw bounding our horizon, and stretching along the plains of Alsace.

I found Basil crouded with strangers of all ranks, and all nations, being, at that period, when general hostility had barred the passes from one country to another, al-

moſt the only ſpot left open for the tranſ-
actions of commerce, the aſylum of the
fugitives, and the dawning negociations of
peace.

The firſt view of Switzerland awakened
my enthuſiaſm moſt powerfully—" At
length," thought I, " am I going to contemplate that intereſting country, of which
I have never heard without emotion!—I
am going to gaze upon images of nature;
images of which the idea has ſo often
ſwelled my imagination, but which my
eyes have never yet beheld.—I am going
to repoſe my wearied ſpirit on thoſe ſublime
objects—to ſooth my deſponding heart with
the hope that the moral diſorder 1 have
witneſſed ſhall be rectified, while I gaze
on nature in all her admirable perfections;
and how delightful a tranſition ſhall I find
in the picture of ſocial happineſs which
Switzerland preſents! I ſhall no longer ſee
liberty

liberty profaned and violated; here she smiles upon the hills, and decorates the vallies, and finds, in the uncorrupted simplicity of this people, a firmer barrier than in the cragginess of their rocks, or the snows of their Glaciers!"

Such were my meditations when I first set my foot on the soil of Switzerland; the scenery of the country more than fulfilled the glowing promise of imagination. With respect to the character and manners of the people, a residence of several weeks at Basil somewhat chilled my enthusiasm: I had frequent opportunities of mixing in their societies, and discerned neither the love of arts, of literature of liberty, or of any earthly good, but money—I heard of nothing but the comparative value of louis, and assignats; and if I had not seen the Rhine rolling its turbulent waves majestically by the windows, I might have fancied

cied myself in 'Change-alley, or the Perron of the Palais Royal.

But if I was disappointed, it was perhaps my own fault, or rather the fault of former travellers. Warmed with enthusiasm for the natural beauties of the country, fancy, which loves the dreams of happiness and perfection, has delighted to associate with those enchanting scenes the charm of congenial society; and to connect with the sublime landscape the higher qualities of mind. Imagination places stock-jobbers and usurers with as much reluctance amidst the grandeur of Swifs scenery, as it would fill with a misshapen Gothic image the niche of a Grecian temple. It must be indeed admitted, that the love of gold is a taste pretty generally diffused throughout Europe; that neither the inhabitants of Paris nor of London can be taxed with any remarkable indifference for riches; nor have wealthy persons in either of those capitals any reason to complain of the neglect of their fellow citizens. But although the people of most countries are, with respect to the researches of gain, burghers of Basil, during the hours of the morning, the evening at least is devoted to amusement, to social pleasure, to friendship, to some object that cheers, or sooths the heart, and the projects of interest are laid aside till the morrow. At Basil alone, the toils of trade find no relaxation; they begin with the day, but do not finish at its close; since even the hours of recreation are made subservient to the views of interest; and the only species of amusement in which the burghers of that city indulge themselves, is one at which they can arrange their commercial dealings, strike bargains, and vigorously pursue that main chance which appears to be, their "being's end, and aim."

With thofe views, the men have formed themfelves into different focieties, called *tabagies*, or fmoking-clubs; becaufe all the members fmoke moft furioufly. Each club is compofed of nearly the fame age, a cuftom to which the love of equality perhaps gave rife, but which is obferved to be extremely prejudicial to the manners of the young men of Bafil, by excluding all forms of deference and politenefs, as well as all means of improvement. With refpect to thefe things, there is indeed nothing peculiar to the clubs of Bafil; fince from Brooke's, compofed of the honourable members of the Britifh parliament, to thefe tabagies, filled with the fenators of the laudable Helvetic Body, a man who has long frequented fuch meetings becomes entirely unfit for all other fociety; he foon thinks it an hardfhip to pafs an evening elfewhere, and terms all other company conftraint, becaufe it wants the eafe of a tavern, where tumult is miftaken for

for gaiety, and familiarity for friendship. But while in other places the taste for clubs is confined to a few persons, Basil is a town of clubbists, containing no less than twelve smoking societies, each composed of about sixty members, who meet every afternoon at an early hour, drink tea amidst the exhilarating fumes of tobacco, discuss the political situation, but far more indefatigably the commercial affairs of the town, calculate the gains and losses of the day, form new schemes of acquiring wealth, and separate at the hour of supper before they have said one word on any subject of taste, or literature.

The ladies of Basil, abandoned by the men, have recourse to clubs also, and sometimes twenty ladies assemble together without one man being of the party, although to such as present themselves, admittance, far from being refused, is even gratefully accorded;

corded; and sometimes a stranger taking advantage of the posture of affairs at Basil, which leads a coterie of young handsome women to consider his company as a favour, pays his homage to the ladies, while clouds of other incense are rising in every quarter of the town from the tabagies where their absent husbands are convened.

The female societies of Basil are formed from infancy of children of the same age, and of the same class; and during their childhood the equality of years is so strictly observed in these societies, that sisters, whose ages differ three or four years, have their separate coteries in the same house. There is something soothing in the idea of these infant associations; it seems forming another barrier for our helpless sex, against the future tempests of the world; and no doubt many a fair member of these young societies, when assailed by those storms of misfortune,

fortune, which often beat with the moſt pitileſs fury againſt hearts that can leaſt reſiſt their violence, recalls with tender regret the ſocial circle of her childhood; and perhaps finds in the ſympathy of ſome female companion, to whom ſhe is endeared by the charm of thoſe early recollections, a ſource of conſolation and relief. The young unmarried women, and the dowagers, have all their diſtinct circles, ſometimes increaſed by the admiſſion of ſiſters-in-law, who become part of the family, and ſometimes by the introduction of accidental acquaintances.

They aſſemble by invitation ſucceſſively at each other's houſes, uſually at three in the afternoon; an hour which, though morning with reſpect to dinner, and all the buſy occupations of life at London and Paris, finds the day far advanced at Baſil; where dinner is ſerved, when it is noon, by the clocks of that city, which, for ſeveral centuries

turies paft, have kept the van-guard of time, and for fome reafon, forgotten in the lapfe of ages, probably becaufe not worth being remembered, ftrike twelve in defiance of common fenfe and convenience, when the folar fhadow points eleven.

The ladies prefent themfelves at their coteries with their work-bags upon their arms, and work and converfation begin together; the latter turns, as in other uninftructed minds, upon the every-day goffip of ordinary life. When the domeftic detail of houfhold anecdote, and the tattle of town fcandal fail, they haften to cards—what other refource is left? Time cannot be filled up, as it often is in mixed focieties, by the flutter of coquetry, and the arts of affectation on one fide, and by the offices of galantry, or the ftare of libertinifm on the other

" Where none admire, 'tis ufelefs to excel;
" Where none are Beaux, 'tis vain to be a Belle."

At thefe affemblies the place of honor is at the window, to which in every houfe at Bafil convex mirrors are fixed, and give a view of all that is paffing in the ftreets to a confiderable diftance. Thefe mirrors, confulted every moment by the ladies of Bafil, not to view themfelves, but their neighbours, would have furnifhed Thomfon, had he lived in that city, with another image in his caftle of indolence, of the means of murdering time.

Tea is brought at four in the afternoon, accompanied by an handfome collation, confifting of paftry, fruits, creams, and fweetmeats, and often of ham, and other cold meats. This fubftantial kind of refrefhment is not found unacceptable after a very copious dinner, and with the perfpective of a folid fupper; the Swifs in general being poffeffed of a moft powerful appetite, perhaps arifing from the keennefs of their mountain

mountain air. A dull game of commerce drags on the lingering hours till eight in the evening, when the ladies feparate, after a profufion of compliments, which they have not yet relinquifhed for the French mode of gliding out of the room.

Sometimes their Liege-Lords, the clubbifts, make a facrifice of one dear evening of fmoke and ftock-jobbing, to the women; on thefe gala occafions, the card-party concludes with a fupper, fufficiently luxurious, but which might be more amufing; and as the law forbids any carriages to roll through the ftreets after eleven, the company ufually feparate at that hour.

Fathers and mothers of families, who have children married, fix one day of the week, which they call *leur jour de famille*, when all their offspring affemble at their houfe at dinner, fometimes to the fourth, fifth,

fifth, and even sixth generation; for the women marry very young, and not long since there were not less than six ladies in Basil, whose grand-children were grand-mothers. There is something respectable, and even affecting in these patriarchal meetings; they seem a means of drawing closer those ties of consanguinity which are the best refuge against human ills; in which the purest affections of the heart mingle themselves with the wants and weakness of our nature; guiding with watchful tenderness the wanderings of youth, and supporting with unwearied care the feebleness of age.

The public amusements of Basil were suspended by the magistrates, we were told, on account of the public calamities; the chief of which was the dearness of provisions: an evil the more easily to be borne, as the town was then reaping an

abundant

abundant harveſt of gold from the calamities of other countries. Once a week indeed, the dulneſs of a card aſſembly was permitted to replace that of the coteries; and an occaſional concert harmonized the ſoul; but dancing was a diverſion too light for the times, and even a ſet of dancing-dogs, offending againſt the ſtatute, were formally expelled by the *Chaſſe-Coquin,* probably in conſequence of the general order of the Commiſſion of Six, inſtituted at that period for clearing the town of unprofitable ſtrangers.

CHAP.

CHAP. II.

Comparative View of the Spirit of Commerce in France, before, and since the Revolution.—Paper System.—Female Traders and Contractors.

IN France, a country so near Switzerland in its geographical situation, but so distant in the character and disposition of the people, things in this respect are managed better; and although the French are lately become in some sort also a nation of usurers and stock-jobbers, their mode of toiling for wealth, and their mode of spending it, are altogether different from the plodding usages of their neighbours.

The revolution which destroyed monarchy in France, overthrew at the same time the empire of ancient prejudices and habits. Before that event, vanity was the governing spring of French action, and the principal aim, and aliment of that vanity, was rank and titles. A trader only laboured to procure juft money enough to purchafe a charge of treafurer of France, or *fecretaire du roi*, and when thus honourably ennobled, confidered it as beneath his dignity to continue any longer that commerce which had ferved as the ftep-ladder to his elevation.

But the fcene is now reverfed. Nobility exifts no longer, and opinions have undergone as great a revolution as titles and fortunes. The poor are enriched; the rich are impoverifhed; labour is become neceffary; induftry flourifhes on the ruins of vanity; and, as the impetuous French are ever in extremes, their ancient difdain of mercantile occupations is fucceeded by a fort of rage for commerce. To this new fury they are animated, not only by the call of neceffity, but by the defire of enjoyment. This people, the ever ardent lovers of pleafure, pant to repair thofe moments

ments of terror and desolation which were lost to their accustomed, their beloved gaieties. They seek amusement with new eagerness, and the dangers which they find attendant on a revolution, only serve to attach them more to the present moment, on the Epicurean principle of uncertainty respecting the future.

Immense commercial resources are found in the fertility, the extent, the situation, and the wants of the French Republic; but nothing can be more amusing than the various whimsical directions into which the active, restless genius of the people, have turned their present rage for traffic. All grasp at something strange, and something great; a new world seems opening to their view, and which all model after their own fashion. Every man has seized upon some profound discovery, some happy speculation, which will infallibly pour forth an

ever-flowing stream of inexhaustible wealth.
When one chimera fails, another swiftly
springs up; all is " bubble, bubble, toil
and trouble;" spurred by hope, or goaded
by want, every man mounts the hobby-
horse of his imagination, and whips it up
to some marvellous atchievement.

One citizen frames stoves of paper more
durable than brass or steel; another erects
mills that scorn the aid of fire, wind, or
water; another extracts new chemical sub-
stances, which, when applied to commerce,
are to produce riches beyond the visions of
the alchemists. All announce that they
have set their inventive talents upon the
anvil, merely for the good of their country;
and as the ideas which the revolution has
awakened, have given every individual in
France some floating notions of his own
importance, every man, however ignorant
or mistaken, boldly brings forward his infallible

fallible plan, infifts upon his right of being heard by his fellow-citizens, and calls upon every capitalift to haften to him with his funds, and calculate, if he can, the enormous mafs of intereft with which the wings of every moment will be loaded.

Thofe who decline fetting up as inventors, and enlightening the world by difcoveries, although they refufe to travel through unknown tracts of commercial enterprize, at leaft engage in more beaten paths of gain. Throughout the wide extent of the Republic, Gothic abbies are transformed into manufactories, cloifters become work-fhops, chapels are converted into warehoufes, the receffes of folitary fuperftition are invaded, and the hollow echoes of the long-refounding aifles, which were once only refponfive to the folemn flow-breathed chant, now repeat the rude diffonance of the workman's tools. A ftrange confufion of images is excited in the mind by the prefent contemplation of thefe antique edifices, which imagination has been accuftomed to appropriate to congenial inhabitants, pacing filently along their vaulted paffages in floating garments, inftead of which you now meet the barearmed, brawny artificer, and all ideas of folemn ftillnefs vanifh amidft the rude gabble of his noify brood. No doubt an artifan is far more ufeful than a monk, but he looks much lefs picturefque when placed beneath a ruined arch, and gazed at in perfpective.

While fpeculators in the country are converting abbies into manufactories, fpeculators in Paris are perhaps, on a furer principle of calculation, transforming palaces into reforts of public amufement, fo new, fo various, and fo Grecian in all their plans
and

and defignations, that to trace a flight fketch of them will require one of our whole following chapters.

The fyftem of paper-money contributed to cherifh the new fpirit of fpeculation in France, by fuffering the imagination to rove amidft ideal regions of vifionary wealth. The moft trifling purchafe or tranfaction, at that period, had fomething in it of founding greatnefs; a pair of fhoes coft a thoufand livres, an ell of ribband five hundred; and as the women in France have even more active fpirits than the men, every lady who had fifty, or a hundred thoufand livres in her pocket-book, confidered herfelf as a fort of capitalift; and hearing inceffantly from all parts, and in all directions, that commerce was the infallible road to wealth, immediately fet up with thofe folid funds fome fpecies of trade. One lady provided herfelf herself with a cargo of pocket handkerchiefs, another with an aſſortment of ſhoes; ſome ſold tallow-candles, ſome wax; ſome dealt in powder, and others in ſnuff; but all had their little traffic, all were animated by the ſame reſtleſs ſpirit of gain. This ſpecies of commerce, however, was of fleeting duration. Sterne has obſerved, that Frenchmen conceive, better than they combine; ſtill more juſtly may this obſervation be applied to French women; who, when they became adventurers in the new world of traffic, exulted in the rapid augmentation of their wealth; and were aſtoniſhed to find that the merchandize, which was to replace the ſtock, could no longer be purchaſed with the ſame capital; till at length they diſcovered, that their magnificent commercial profits were a ſort of fairy-gold, which, when touched, turned to ſand; and that it was not

the

the merchandize which had increased in price, but the assignats that had diminished in value.

A few of the most beautiful, and the most intriguing of the fair Parisians, became the agents and emissaries of their friends, lovers, or husbands, in the public offices; and the marine, the war, and the home-departments, were filled with female contractors and negociators, who, for the most part, found that republican committees made no better defence than polished courts, against the formidable artillery of bright eyes, gay smiles, lively sallies, and animated graces; artillery which French women know better how to wield, than the women of any other country. Ministers and commissaries felt the energy of arguments uttered by ruby lips, and the claims of a petition offered by a soft hand, of which the naked well-shaped arm was
grace-

gracefully stretched out; and, upon the whole, the women of France, to whom, by the Constitutional Act, all rights have been denied, find that they still hold a tolerably despotic empire over their lords and masters, the sovereign people.

Of a different class from these female negociators and merchants, were those women, who, once possessed of all that rank and fortune could bestow, were now reduced to supply the pressing wants of the moment, by a melancholy species of traffic; by selling various pieces of ornamental needle-work, which they had once been taught to execute as an amusement, or by making a profession of those arts which they had once acquired as the accomplishments of an elegant education. Above all, drawing has proved an useful resource in these circumstances. Many a lady has found in her pencil, a means of subsistence for herself and family;

many a finifhed landfcape, deftined to grace a cryftal *boudoir*, or decorate a gilded pavillion, has ferved to furnifh the fair artift with the cruft of bread which, in fome lonely garret, fhe moiftens with her tears. What a long and mournful page of tranfitions the domeftic annals of a revolution contain!

CHAP. III.

Amusements of Paris.—Balls.—Festivals.—Supper given by a Contractor.—Dress.—Parallel between a Contractor and a Stock-holder.—New Aristocracy.—Modern Royalists.—Odeon.—Bals à la Victime.—Tivoli.—Elysium.—Bagatelle and other Public Gardens.—Glaciers of Paris:

IF the morning at Paris is devoted to business, the evening at least belongs to pleasure: over those hours she holds an undivided empire, but is worshipped at innumerable altars, and hailed by ever-varying rituals.

During the last winter the amusements of twenty-four theatres, which were opened every night, were every night succeeded by public and private balls, in such numbers, that there were no less than two thousand ball-rooms inscribed on the registers of the police, which keeps its wakeful vigils over every sort of amusement, in all their gradations, from the bright blaze of waxen tapers which displays the charms of nymphs dressed

STATE OF SWITZERLAND. 29

dreſſed *à la ſauvage,* or *à la grec,* who grace the ſplendid ball *de Richlieu;* to the oily lamp which lights up the ſeventh ſtory, or the vaulted cellar, where the blind fidler's animating ſcrape calls the ſovereign people to the cotillon of wooden ſhoes.

Theſe two thouſand ball-rooms of the capital afford ample proof that no revolution has taken place in the manners of the French, and that they are ſtill a dancing nation. They have indeed of late fully demonſtrated to the world that they are capable of greater things; and that when the energies of their ſouls are called forth, they can follow Buonaparte acroſs the bridge of Lodi; but when their minds return to their natural poſition, every barrack has a room appropriated for dancing, and the heroes of Arcole, as well as the *muſcadins* of Paris,

"All knit hands, and beat the ground
"In a light fantaſtic round."

The

The fetes of the court, it is afferted by the few perfons remaining in France, by whom they were frequented, were but tawdry fplendour compared with the claffical elegance which prevails at the fetes of our republican contractors. As a fpecimen of thefe private balls, I fhall trace a fhort fketch of a dance lately given by one of the furnifhers of ftores for fleets and armies, in his fpacious hotel, where all the furniture, in compliance with the prefent fafhion at Paris, is antique; where all that is not Greek is Roman; where ftately filken beds, maffy fophas, worked tapeftry, and gilt ornaments, are thrown afide as rude Gothic magnificence, and every couch refembles that of Pericles, every chair thofe of Cicero; where every wall is finifhed in arabefque, like the baths of Titus, and every table, upheld by Caftors and Polluxes, is covered with Athenian bufts and Etrufcan vafes; where that modern piece of furniture a clock is concealed

concealed beneath the classic bar of Phœbus, and the dancing hours; and every chimney-iron is supported by a Sphinx, or a Griffin. The dress of his female visitors was in perfect harmony with the furniture of his hotel; for although the Parisian ladies are not suspected of any obstinate attachment to Grecian modes of government, they are most rigid partizans of Grecian modes of dress, adorned like the contemporaries of Aspasia—the loose light drapery, the naked arm, the bare bosom, the sandaled feet, the circling zone, the golden chains, the twisting tresses, all display the most inflexible conformity to the laws of republican costume. The most fashionable hairdresser of Paris in order to accommodate himself to the classical taste of his fair customers is provided with a variety of antique busts as models; and when he waits on a lady, enquires if she chuses to be dreft that day *à la Cleopatre, la Dianne,* or *la Psyche?*

Pfyche? Sometimes the changeful nymph is a veſtal, ſometimes a Venus; but the laſt rage has been the *Niobé*, of late fat and lean, gay and grave, old and young, have been all *à la Niobé*; and the many-curled periwig, thrown aſide by the faſhionable claſs, now decorates the heads of pretty ſhop-keepers.

The fair Grecians being determined not to injure the contour of fine forms by ſuperfluous incumbrances, no faſhionable lady at Paris wears any pockets, and the inconvenience of being without is obviated by ſticking her fan in her belt, ſliding in a flat purſe of morocco leather, only large enough to contain a few louis, at the ſide of her neck, and giving her ſnuff-box and her pocket-handkerchief to the care of the gentleman who attends her, and to whom ſhe applies for them whenever ſhe has occaſion.

For a short time during the winter, in defiance of frost and snow, the costume of a few reigning belles was not *à la grec,* but *a la sauvage.* To be dressed *à la sauvage,* was to have all that part of the frame which was not left uncovered clad in a light drapery of flesh colour. The boddice under which no linen was worn (shifts being an article of dress long since rejected at Paris, both by the Greeks and the Savages) the boddice was made of knitted silk, clinging exactly to the shape, which it perfectly displayed; the petticoat was on one side twisted up by a light festoon; and the feet, which were either bare or covered with a silk stocking of flesh colour, so woven as to draw upon the toes like a glove upon the fingers, were decorated with diamonds. These gentle savages, however, found themselves so rudely treated whenever they appeared, by the sovereign multitude, that at length the fashions of Otaheite were thrown aside, and Greece remains the standing order of the day.

But to return to the contractor, and his ball—after several hours had past in dancing cotillons, which the young women of Paris perform with a degree of perfection—a light nymphish grace unseen elsewhere—and after the walse, which is now never forgotten at a Paris ball, had proved that the steady heads of Niobés were not to be made giddy, the company were led to a supper furnished with Eastern magnificence, and decorated with attic taste. After supper the folding doors of the saloon were thrown open to a garden of considerable extent, beautifully illuminated with coloured lamps, and its trees bending with lavish clusters of fruits of every season, and every climate, formed of ice, while fountains poured forth streams of orgeat, lemonade, and liqueurs.

But

But while thefe imitators of Greece and Rome are revelling in Afiatic luxury, you hear them lamenting moft pathetically the fubverfion of the ancient regime; that regime, which would at leaft have had thus much of juftice, that it would have retained thefe perfonages in the anti-chambers of the faloons they now occupy; to which antichambers they would with a counter-revolution moft probably return. One is obliged to offer up an invocation to patience, when condemned to liften to their declamations againft that new order of things to which folely they owe their elevation.

There is indeed one clafs of perfons, before whofe complaints of the revolution, however bitter, the mind humbles itfelf in fympathetic forrow. The poor *rentier*, while he fips his Spartan black-broth, which he is forced to procure by parting, in fad gradation, with all the relicks of his former

former splendour, with watches, rings, furniture, and clothes: he indeed if he complains, is to be pitied, and if he forbears complaint, is to be revered! But alas, there is so much of tragical detail in the pages of the *great book;* a thing which has long since been called a great evil, that we must give it at least a whole chapter to itself.

At present I shall only observe, that the reign of terror has acted upon this country like some mighty pestilence, which not only sweeps away devoted millions in its fury but leaves an obnoxious taint upon every object where it has passed. The reign of terror has given a fatal wound to the energies of public spirit; ordinary minds have mistaken the execrable abuses of liberty for an effect of the generous principle itself: the victims of revolutionary government have lifted up their complaining voice; all the emotions of sympathy, and all the feelings

ings of indignation have been called forth; and the partizans of the ancient regime have left no art unpractifed, no feduction untried, to take advantage of thefe difpofitions in favor of their own fyftem.

Thofe who have been too rapidly enriched by the revolution have endeavoured to hide the obfcurity of their origin, by mimicking the tones of thofe who have titles and honors to regret, till ariftocracy has defcended fo low, that it will foon perhaps be exploded, like any other fafhion, when taken up by the vulgar. Many of the fair wives of titled emigrants or blooming widows of murdered nobles, who have made fuch fecond marriages, that we might well apoftrophize them in the language of Hamlet:

"Such an act
"That blurs the grace and blufh of modefty,
"Calls virtue hypocrite,
"Makes marriage vows
"As falfe as Dicers' oaths."

These very ladies, who have taught their new-made Liege-Lords to ape their counter-revolutionary follies, will at length be ashamed of their aristocracy, when they find how successfully they are rivalled in those sentiments by their milliners and mantua-makers. A writer of a late political pamphlet has given an admirable reason why our Parisian belles will soon lay aside the tone of eternal lamentations for the overthrow of despotism. "Seven years," says he, "have already elapsed since the epocha of the revolution: seven years is a period of some length in the history of a youthful beauty, and a lady will soon not be able to regret the monarchy under the penalty of passing for old." I believe every person who has studied the female heart, will agree with this writer, that the republic has a tolerable chance upon this principle of obtaining ere long many fair proselytes.

The fans, sparkling with spangled *fleurs de lys*, will then be broken; the rings, bearing the insignia of royalty, will be melted down; and the *porte-feuilles*, and *bon-bonnieres*, with their sliding-lids, displaying the forbidden images of regal greatness, will no longer be borne about in a sort of triumphal manner, not from a sentiment of sorrow, by those who, attendant on their persons, and basking in their smiles, are privileged to display more than that general regret for their unhappy destiny which humanity feels; but from a sensation of vanity by those, who perhaps never breathed the same atmosphere; never, even at awful distance, gazed upon the originals of those pictures which they now affect to cherish as the tender memorials of peculiar favor. These relicks, we may venture to predict, will be offered up in one mighty sacrifice at the shrine of the republic, the moment it is well underſtood that to be a republican, is to be young.

Public balls, as well as concerts, were held laſt winter at the *Theatre Français*, which, after having been long ſhut up, was repaired, embelliſhed, and baptized by the Greek name of the *Odeon;* and that no jealouſy might exiſt between the balls and concerts, on account of this claſſical nomenclature, the balls immediately received the appellation of *thiaſes.*

But the moſt ſingular ſpecies of amuſement which the laſt winter produced, were ſubſcription-balls, entiled *des bals à la victime.* Such, and ſo powerful was the rage for pleaſure, that a certain number of its votaries, who, during the tyranny of Robeſpierre, had loſt their neareſt relations on the ſcaffold, inſtituted, not days of ſuch ſolemn,

solemn, sad commemoration, as is dear to the superstition of tenderness, when, in melancholy procession, clad in sable, and wreathed with cypress, they might have knelt, a mourning multitude, around the spot where the mutilated bodies of their murdered parents had been thrown by the executioner; and bathed the sod with those bitter tears which filial affection, or agonized love, shed over the broken ties of nature, or of passion—no!—the commemorative rites which these mourners offered to the manes of their massacred relations, were festive balls! To these strange, unhallowed orgies, no one could be admitted who had not lost a father, a mother, a husband, a wife, a brother, or a sister, on the guillotine; but any person with a certificate of their execution in his pocket-book, not only obtained admission, but might dance as long, and as merrily as heart could wish. Had Holben been present at such a spectacle, no doubt he would have

have enriched his death-dance with new images, and led forward each gay nymph by an attendant headless spectre. The indignant cry of public opinion, however, was at length heard above the music of the walse and the cotillon; and the *bal à la victime* exists no longer to bear its powerful testimony to a depravation, not merely of manners, but of the heart.

If in the winter, conformably to our Grecian ideas at Paris, concert-rooms became *Odeons*, and the Niobés and the Titus's danced in a *thiase*, summer can boast of more than equal honors; since then we never tread but on attic ground, and never suffer ourselves to be pleased but when pleasure presents herself with a classical appellation. Witness ye gardens of Tivoli, ye bowers of Idalia, ye winding walks of Elysium, ye grottos of Venus, ye vales of Tempe, ye groves of Thessaly! witness

with

with what fond alacrity the lovers of antiquity fly in multitudes to your enchanting recesses, where the arching trees are hung with innumerable lamps of varying colours, where the ear is exhilarated with the sounds of music, and the eye is cheared with the movements of the dance; and where every evening the hour of ten serves as a general signal, at which the whole city of Paris seems one vast theatre for the display of fireworks. A stranger who should enter this city at night by the bridge of Neuilly, might suppose that he had reached this scene of great events at some important epocha, which had occasioned a general rejoicing. On his right he would discern the lights of *Bagatelle*, beaming through the *Bois de Boulogne*, and would pass close to the brilliant entrance of Idalia; on his left he would be dazzled by the illuminations of the Elysium; while, as he advanced, he would discern, above every quarter

quarter of the town, the tall sky-rockets darting their vivid flash, and would hear in all directions the light explosions of enchanted palaces, with bright arcades and fairy columns;

> " The crackling flames appear on high,
> " And driving sparkles dance along the sky."

Bagatelle alone, the once gay retreat of the Comte d'Artois, is suffered, by our Grecian amateurs, to retain its old appellation in favour of the regal images which it brings to memory. What food for the ramblings of the mind along the paths of history, when it contrasts the light French modern graces of Bagatelle, with the massy, Gothic gloom of Holyrood-House! It may be observed, that the persons who are for ever lamenting the subversion of the ancient regime, are not prevented by their regrets from giving all the encouragement in their power to those who
con-

convert one palace after another into scenes of public amusement; and that they eagerly purchase for half a crown, the privilege of treading gaily every evening with the plebeian multitude, those magnificent gardens and sumptuous hotels, of which the possessors have, for the most part, as in former proscriptions, paid for their beautiful retreats at Alba, with their lives. But while these lovers of despotism forget their regrets in their pleasures, the philosophic mind wanders often in musing mood along these festive haunts, where the most singular combinations croud upon reflection; and, amist the glowing enthusiasm of liberty,* mourns those partial evils that have clouded its brightness, and abhors those cruel abuses that have sullied its cause!

When the multiplied engagements of the evening do not offer leisure for an excursion to Tivoli, or a trip to Idalia, the gay world

at

at leaſt find ſufficient time in the interval between the play and the *petit ſouper*, to lounge for half an hour at one of the faſhionable *glaciers*. A glacier is a ſort of coffee-houſe, eſtabliſhed in the fine hotels of emigrants, ſplendidly illuminated, open to perſons of both ſexes, and where you pay for your admiſſion by eating ices, for which there is now ſo extraordinary a demand in Paris, that if the following winter ſhould prove mild, the ice-purveyors will perhaps be forced to ſend to the department of Mont Blanc, in order to furniſh themſelves with means of ſupplying the enormous wants of their cuſtomers.

But let me recall the images moſt dear to my imagination, by leaving for a while the glaciers of Paris, and the ſmoking-clubs of Baſil, and wandering amidſt the ſublime landſcapes of Switzerland. How delightful to bid adieu to every-day occurrences, occupations, cares, and pleafures, for the contemplation of thofe fcenes of folemn grandeur, which form fuch a contraft to the littlenefs of ordinary life ! Let me turn my fteps towards the firft auguft object which ftruck my eye in Switzerland, the cataract of the Rhine at Schaffhaufen, to which place I was obliged to travel by a long circuitous route to Zurich, fince with French paffports the Auftrian territory was forbidden ground. A Balois told me before my departure, that the cataract of the Rhine was fcarcely worth fo much trouble; fince, " after all," faid he, " it is but a fall of water !"

CHAP. IV.

Road from Basil into the Canton of Soleure.—Swiss Taste in Gardening.—Visit to a Farm-house.—Rural Ceremonies.—Traditionary Story of the Destruction of a Tyrant.—Baden.—Zurich.—Reflections on the View over the Lake to the Alps.—Fall of the Rhine at Lauffen.—Bridge at Schaffhausen.

THROUGH what a delicious country we passed in travelling along the Canton of Basil to that of Soleure! What beautiful, what various combinations of rock, pine-clad hills thrown together in noble masses, and richly covered with their dark-tinted verdure; above which a bare peak sometimes lifts its sharp spiral head, as if to give effect to the landscape.

What grateful sounds to my ear were the murmurs of those soothing cascades, and clear rills which had more of beauty than sublimity,

sublimity, but which filled my heart with emotion, while I considered them as the prelude of scenes, where the water-fall swells into a torrent, and where, instead of rapid brooks, and small streams, the broad lake spreads its majestic expanse of waters.

I was yet only in the vestibule of Switzerland, and nature appeared to me as if lifting up gradually the veil which concealed those mighty objects of overwhelming grandeur, which my imagination sprung forward to meet with enthusiastic rapture. We passed by several country houses, with pleasure-grounds covered with verdant seats, bowers, and arbours, profanely cut into all the mishapen forms of Gothic fury, and where literally,

" Grove nods at grove, each alley has a brother,
" And half the platform justs reflects the other."

One might forgive a Dutchman for clipping his trees, and squaring his walks by the same rule with which he cuts his canals, and digs his ditches; but here, in the very temple of nature, where the inhabitant has but to cast his eye around him in order to learn all that she can teach of grace and majesty, it seems difficult to avoid feeling, that *jets-d'eaux* are but ludicrous mimickry in the neighbourhood of cataracts, that bouquets of yew, and pillars of fir, lose much of their effect when placed beneath hanging woods of pines, and columns of cliffs, and that the romantic hills above are an eternal satire on the trim walks below.

In our way to Schaffhausen, we spent some agreeable days with a small party, at a farm-house in the Canton of Basil, situated in the nook of a mountain. High hills rise sloping round this little white dwelling, covered with fine pasturage, and scattered

tered over with trees, woody copfes, and fwift rivulets flowing down their green fides. An Irifh gentleman, who had hired apartments in this habitation for the fummer, and whom we went to vifit, had cut winding paths along the fteep hills with his own hands, directed the frefh fprings to flow into cool baths, and placed Italian, Latin, and French infcriptions upon the trees, in the charming receffes of the hanging woods

When our good farmer bought his ground, its appendages of woods, cliffs, and rills, had probably only entered into his fpeculations, fo far as they were the means or the impediments of culture; but an Englifh nobleman would have purchafed them with half his fortune. During our ftay in this beautiful retreat we, lived with the farmer and his family, eat of their bread,

bread, drank of their cup, and found perfect neatnefs, as well as plentiful hofpitality at their table.

The farmer, a plain, honeft, fenfible Swifs, was proud of his country, and above all, proud of his privileges, as he happened to be a burgher of Bafil. He produced a kind of placard, which had been in his family, he faid, for ages; and we obferved that the date was in the middle of the fifteenth century. On this large placard was not ill engraven all the memorable hiftorical events of Switzerland, fince it began its ftruggles for freedom, with poetry below, explaining more fully the atchievements which the painting related above. Our farmer felt his foul animated, and himfelf half a warrior, while he gazed on thefe glorious triumphs of his anceftors. I was, perhaps, the more ftruck with his enthufiafm,

fiafm, becaufe it was the firft time I had observed any such sentiment since my arrival in Switzerland.

In the commercial parts of that country, this feeling of pride in the feats of their progenitors is as completely extinct as the heroic race itself, which is long since gone to the family-vault of all the Capulets; but in the little or ancient Cantons which were the cradle of Swifs liberty, this generous sentiment is still cherished. The peasants teach their children the oral tale of other times, and they early imbibe with the love of their own country an inveterate hatred against Auftria. The memory of those valorous deeds is also impressed on the mind by coarse paintings, which cover the walls of the peasants houses, and are sometimes so large as narrowly to escape the fate of the Vicar of Wakefield's family picture.

The farmer alfo recounted to me fome of the ruftic folemnities which are practifed in the Canton of Bafil, where the peafants crown with heaps of flowers the hive which produces the firft fwarm of bees; and when the cows firft go to grafs in the fpring, and leave it in the autumn, a long proceffion is formed of two cows abreaft, whofe horns are gayly decorated for the gala, aud who are led on by two white cows moft profufely covered with wreaths, and ribbands of various colours. This cuftom, I am told, is as ancient as the days of Theocritus, who talks of adorning his favorite cow with chaplets.

Many a traditionary tale gives a moral intereft to the picturefque fcenes of this enchanting country. In one of our airings on horfeback, during our ftay at the farmhoufe, we paffed through a defile, above which rofe piles of cliffs five hundred feet high,

high, and on the brow of one thofe towering craggs we difcerned the ruins of a Gothic caftle, two windows of which ftill remain. " There," faid our guide, pointing to the frowning fummit of the rock, "fome ages paft lived a tyrant: he delighted in defolation and death, and whenever any of his vaffals offended him, he ordered them to appear before him, and then caufed the unhappy victims to be thrown headlong from yonder horrible precipice into this gulph below. Three centuries fince his vaffals had their revenge; they armed themfelves, climbed up at night by almoft inacceffible paths to the caftle, which they furprized, and fet on fire, and the tyrant perifhed in the flames."

We left, with regret, the farmer's white dwelling, and croffing a part of the chain of Jura, proceeded on our journey to Baden, which is the Bath of Switzerland,
celebrated

celebrated for the virtues of its hot springs, and is much frequented in summer; but there are no public meetings, and the company associate little together. The town is surrounded by lofty green hills; and the Limat flows at their feet with an impetuous rapidity, which seems to realize the poetical idea of living waters. We walked along a narrow path along the edge of the river to a limpid fountain, where the country girls, dressed in the picturesque costume of the female Swiss peasantry, came to draw water, and gave a more pastoral air to the scene. Bidding farewel to Badeu, where we had been received by Mr. Barthelemy, the French Ambassador, with elegant hospitality, we pursued our course to Zuric.

This neat, and chearful town, is divided into two parts by the Limat, and delightfully situated on the northern extremity of
its

its noble lake, which spreads, far as the eye can reach, its mass of limped waters, bounded by vine-covered hills, whose slopes are thick-studded with houses and villages; while beyond this scene of picturesque beauty, the Alps, covered with their eternal snows, rise in the distant perspective, stretching towards the south-west, and mingling their summits with the clouds. It was not without the most powerful emotion that, for the first time, I cast my eyes on that solemn, that majestic vision, the Alps!—how often had the idea of those stupendous mountains filled my heart with enthusiastic awe!—so long, so eagerly, had I desired to contemplate that scene of wonders, that I was unable to trace when first the wish was awakened in my bosom—it seemed from childhood to have made a part of my existence—I longed to bid adieu to the gayly-peopled landscapes of Zuric, and wander amidst those regions of mysterious

subli-

sublimity, the solitudes of nature, where her eternal laws seem at all seasons to forbid more than the temporary visits of man, and where, sometimes, the dangerous passes to her frozen summits are inflexibly barred against mortal footsteps. The pleasure arising from the varying forms of smiling beauty with which we were surrounded, became a cold sensation, while expectation hung upon those vast gigantic shapes, that half-seen chaos which excited the stronger feelings of wonder, mingled with admiration. But I was obliged, with whatever regret, to relinquish for the present a nearer view of those tremendous objects, since private affairs left me only sufficient leisure to visit the cataract of the Rhine before I returned to Basil; whence, however, I soothed myself with the hope of being soon able to depart in search of the terrific scenes of the Alps, and the rich luxuriant graces of the Italian vallies of Switzerland. In the mean time we we paffed haftily through Zuric, in our way to Schaffhaufen, for although I had been affured that the cataract of the Rhine was " but a fall of water," it had excited fo tormenting a curiofity, that I found I fhould be incapable of feeing any thing elfe with pleafure or advantage, till I had once gazed upon that object.

When we reached the fummit of the hill which leads to the fall of the Rhine, we alighted from the carriage, and walked down the fteep bank, whence I faw the river rolling turbulently over its bed of rocks, and heard the noife of the torrent, towards which we were defcending, increafing as we drew near. My heart fwelled with expectation—our path, as if formed to give the fcene its full effect, concealed for fome time the river from our view; till we reached a wooden balcony, projecting on the edge of the water, and whence, juft
fheltered

sheltered from the torrent, it bursts in all its overwhelming wonders on the astonished sight. That stupendous cataract, rushing with wild impetuosity over those broken, unequal rocks, which, lifting up their sharp points amidst its sea of foam, disturb its headlong course, multiply its falls, and make the afflicted waters roar—that cadence of tumultuous sound, which had never till now struck upon my ear—those long feathery surges, giving the element a new aspect—that spray rising into clouds of vapour, and reflecting the prismatic colours, while it disperses itself over the hills—never, never can I forget the sensations of that moment! when with a sort of annihilation of self, with every past impression erased from my memory, I felt as if my heart were bursting with emotions too strong to be sustained.—Oh, majestic torrent! which hast conveyed a new image of nature to my soul, the moments I have passed

passed in contemplating thy sublimity will form an epocha in my short span!—thy course is coeval with time, and thou wilt rush down thy rocky walls when this bosom, which throbs with admiration of thy greatness, shall beat no longer!

What an effort does it require to leave, after a transient glimpse, a scene on which, while we meditate, we can take no account of time! its narrow limits seem too confined for the expanded spirit; such objects appear to belong to immortality; they call the musing mind from all its little cares and vanities, to higher destinies and regions, more congenial than this world to the feelings they excite. I had been often summoned by my fellow-travellers to depart, had often repeated "but one moment more," and many "moments more" had elapsed, before I could resolve to tear myself from the balcony.

We

We croffed the river, below the fall, in a boat, and had leifure to obferve the furrounding fcenery. The cataract, however, had for me a fort of fafcinating power, which, if I withdrew my eyes for a moment, again faftened them on its impetuous waters. In the back-ground of the torrent a bare mountain lifts its head encircled with its blue vapours; on the right rifes a fteep cliff, of an enormous height, covered with wood, and upon its fummit ftands the Caftle of Lauffen, with its frowning towers, and encircled with its crannied wall; on the left, human induftry has feized upon a flender thread of this mighty torrent in its fall, and made it fubfervient to the purpófes of commerce. Founderies, mills, and wheels, are erected on the edge of the river, and a portion of the vaft bafon into which the cataract falls is confined by a dyke, which preferves the warehoufes and the neighbouring huts from its inundations.

Sheltered

STATE OF SWITZERLAND. 63

Sheltered within this little nook, and accustomed to the neighbourhood of the torrent, the boatman unloads his merchandize, and the artisan pursues his toil, regardless of the falling river, and inattentive to those thundering sounds which seem calculated to suspend all human activity in solemn and awful astonishment; while the imagination of the spectator is struck with the comparative littleness of fleeting man, busy with his trivial occupations, contrasted with the view of nature in all her vast, eternal, uncontrolable grandeur *.

We

* Mr. Cox estimates the height of the cataract of the Rhine at only fifty feet; Monf. Ramond, his elegant French translator, adds the following note to this observation:—" The quantity of water, which varies according to the season, has some influence upon the height, and a considerable effect upon the aspects of this fall. Those who have seen it at the period when the snows dissolve, will admit that description to be exact which Mr. Cox thinks exaggerated, and only

true

We walked over the celebrated wooden bridge at Schaffhaufen, of which the bold and fimple conftruction is confidered as an extraordinary effort of genius in the architect. Being altogether unqualified to judge of, or to defcribe its merit, I fhall only obferve, that nature feems to have given the Swifs, together with their rapid rivers, and

true of remote times. I have been affured that the height of the cataract, in thefe circumftances, is not lefs than eighty feet. A ftranger can fcarcely, without temerity, judge from his fimple obfervation, and if he does fo, he will be fure to be below the truth. I have afcertained, and Mr. Cox himfelf makes the fame remark, that it requires the eye of a Swifs to judge of certain dimenfions, which, exceeding all we have before feen, find no model of proportion in the mind. Thofe who have travelled for the firft time in Switzerland, have often found, to their great furprife, that inftead of exaggerating the heights and the diftances, they have diminifhed them one-half, or two-thirds, till long habit taught them to expand their ideas, by furnifhing them with fit objects of comparifon."

their

their torrent ſtreams, an extraordinary genius for erecting bridges, of ſuch daring deſign, hung upon the cliff, and fuſpended over the gulph, that we are not furpriſed to find fuperſtition has fometimes attributed them to fupernatural agency.

Part of our company being furniſhed only with French paſſports, we left Schaffhauſen and returned to Zuric, without having viſited the Lake of Conſtance, or its renowned and ancient city, which, at that period, was peopled by multitudes who had left France without paſſports.

CHAP. V.

Lavater.—Fall of Infidelity, and Triumph of the Religion of our Fathers.—Fashionable Devotees.—La Harpe. —Lectures on Religion at Idalia.—Desertion of the Proselytes.—Theophilanthropism.

WE staid long enough at Zuric to visit its first literary ornament Lavater. It being known that he is willing to receive strangers, no traveller of any lettered curiosity passes through the town, without paying him the homage of a visit.

He received us in his library, which was hung thick with portraits and engravings, of which he has a considerable collection, forming a complete study of the ever varying expression of the human face divine. Some very wise men, who admit of no scope to that faculty of the mind called imagination, and are for ever bringing every

every theory to the fquare, and the compafs, confider his fyftem of phyfiognomy as the fantaftic vifion of an heated brain; but though it may be difficult, it is furely ingenious and interefting to attempt reducing to rules a fcience, which feems to be founded in nature. It is furely curious to analyfe what it is fo eafy to feel, the charm of that expreffion, which is the emanation of moral qualities; that undefinable grace which is not beauty, but fomething more; without which its enchantments lofe their power of fafcination, and which can fhed an animated glow, a fpark of divinity over the features of deformity:

" Mind, mind alone, bear witnefs earth, and heaven,
" The living fountain in itfelf contains
" Of beauteous and fublime."

Lavater is a venerable looking old man, with a fharp long face, high features, and a wrinkled brow: he is tall, thin, and interefting interesting in his figure; when serious he has a look of melancholy, almost of inquietude; but when he smiles, his countenance becomes lighted up with an expression of sweetness and intelligence.

There is a simple eloquence in his conversation, an effusion of the heart extremely attractive: he speaks French with some difficulty, and whenever he is at a loss for an expression has recourse to German, which I in vain begged a Swiss gentleman, who was of our party, to translate for me: he told me that for the most part the German words Lavater employed were compound-epithets of his own framing, which had peculiar energy as he used them, but which would be quite vapid and spiritless in translation.

The great rule of moral conduct, Lavater said, in his opinion, was, next to God, to respect refpect time. Time, he confidered as the moft valuable of human treafures, and any wafte of it as in the higheft degree immoral. He rifes every morning at the hour of five; and though it would be agreeable to him to breakfaft immediately after rifing, makes it an invariable rule to earn that repaft by fome previous labour; fo that if by accident the reft of the day is fpent to no ufeful purpofe, fome portion of it may at leaft be fecured beyond the interruptions of chance.

Lavater gave us a moft pleafing account of morals in Zuric. He had been a preacher of the gofpel, he faid, in that town thirty years; and fo incapable were the citizens of any fpecies of corruption, that he fhould have rendered himfelf ridiculous had he ever during that long period preached a fermon againft it, fince it was a vice unknown. " At what a diftance," thought

thought I, " am I arrived from London and Paris."

When we took our leave of Lavater, he begged we would write our names and place of abode in a book, which he appropriates to the ufe of infcribing the long lift of his foreign vifitors. An hour after my return from his houfe he came to pay me a vifit, which I was taught to confider as an unufual compliment, fince it is his general rule not to return the vifits of ftrangers. Religion was the theme of his difcourfe, and he talked of its pleafures, its confolations, and its hopes, with a folemn fort of enthufiaftic fervor, which fhewed how much his heart was interefted in the fub_ject, and how warmly his fenfibility was awake to devotional feelings. Although his zeal was not without knowledge, yet it was fomewhat difficult to difcover what was his fyftem of belief: whether he was of Paul

Paul or Apollos, a follower of Calvin according to the established creed of the Swiss church, or whether he was not in some sort the framer of a new doctrine himself.

One of my fellow-travellers, who was anxious to wrest from the venerable pastor his confession of faith, brought in review before him the various opinions of the fathers, orthodox and heretic; from Justin Martyr and Origin, down to the Bishop of St. David's and Dr. Priestley. But Lavater did not appear to have made polemics his study; he seemed to think right and wrong, in historical fact, of far less importance than right and wrong in religious sentiment; and above all, in human action. There was more of feeling than of logic in his conclusions; and he appeared to have taken less pains to examine religion, than to apply its precepts to the regulation of those frailties and passions of the human heart,

heart, the traces of which, hidden from others, he had marked with such admirable accuracy in the character and expreſſion of outward forms. For myſelf, I own the ſolemn, meek, affectionate expreſſion of Lavater's pious ſentiments, were peculiarly ſoothing to my feelings, after having been ſo long ſtunned with the cavils of French philoſophers, or rather the impertinent comments of their diſciples, who are ſo proud of their ſcepticiſm, that they are for ever obtruding it in converſation. The number of thoſe diſciples is augmented ſince the revolution, which has ſpread far and wide the writings of Rouſſeau and Voltaire; and every Frenchman, after having read thoſe authors, though he may neither have taſte enough to admire the charms of their genius, or virtue to feel the philanthropy of their ſentiments, has, at leaſt, acquired ſufficient knowledge to aſſume the appellation of philoſopher, and prove his claim

claim to that title by enlisting himself under the banner of infidelity; without knowing the use of his arms.

This irreverence for religion, however, which Mr. Burke considered as one of the primary causes of the French Revolution, is not, as heretofore, the ton amongst persons of former rank and fashion; infidelity has been in disgrace with that class, ever since it was profaned by the vulgar Jacobin touch; and the only distinguished trophies that system can now boast, are a few Anti-Newtonian flights with respect to final causes, from astronomic infidels. The aristocracy were no sooner convinced that the Catholic establishment, and above all, the non-juring priests were their best auxiliaries, than all the elegant women of Paris became immediately devotees, and nothing was heard of in fashionable saloons but professions of attachment and respect *" pour*

la

la religion de nos peres; by which it was well underſtood that " more was meant than met the ear," and that theſe ſentiments included the government, as well as the creed of their fathers.

The great director of the conſciences of theſe fair converts, dreſt *à la Pſyche*, was Monſ. de la Harpe, a literary man of conſiderable infidel reputation under the old regime; the diſciple and friend of Voltaire, d'Alembert, Diderot, and other eminent encyclypodiſts, and in ſome ſort a leader of the ſect after their deceaſe, or, according to their own creed, after their annihilation. The Gamaliel of Monſ. La Harpe, was Madame C―― T――; it was at her feet, in the gloom of a priſon, during the terrific tyranny of the Jacobins, that this philoſopher was brought to the knowledge and belief of Chriſtianity. I have before obſerved, that the nobleſt examples

amples of fortitude and resignation under sufferings were, during revolutionary government, displayed by women. It was, no doubt, in the calmness and imperturbability of Madame C—— T——'s mind, under the certain expectation of the scaffold, that Monf. La Harpe was first led to admire the effects of a persuasion, which her eloquence and his own conviction made him afterwards adopt; and of which he became, in defiance of all his former opinions, the zealous and fashionable advocate.

The cruel persecution which the Catholic religion had sustained from the intolerant Jacobins, had produced the usual effect of persecution, that of rekindling the pious zeal of a great portion of the people of France. They returned to the religion of their fathers, not from the same motives as those which influenced the fine ladies and gentlemen

gentlemen of Paris, becaufe it was connected with regal government; but becaufe, wearied with revolutionary calamities, they ftood in need of the foothing confolations of devotion; and the churches became crouded places of refort.

It was not, however, in thofe religious temples that the illuftrious convert to the Catholic faith, Monf. La Harpe, became a preacher of its doctrines. Like the hero of Mr. Greaves's novel, Monf. La Harpe took courage to attack the devil in his ftrongeft holds. Being a perfon of high literary merit, he had been chofen to fill the rhetorical chair in the Lyceum. From that place, where, a few moons before, he had defcanted on the glorious conquefts of philofophy over fuperftition, and of liberty and the rights of man over defpotifm and flavery; he now poured forth the recantation of his errors in fo eloquent and touching

ing a ſtrain, that the neighbouring ſquare and ſtreets re-echoed the long and tumultuous applauſes of his fair auditory, for the majority were always ladies.

The lecturer, not ſatisfied with the victory gained over infidelity in this feat of ſcience, of which it had been ſo long in poſſeſſion, purſued that pernicious ſyſtem into another of its fortreſſes, the regions of pleaſure. Monſ. La Harpe, becoming a Catholic, was too ſingular an event not to attract general notice; and as Catholiciſm happened to be in faſhion, the proprietors of various places of amuſement thought a few lectures from Monſ. La Harpe, on "the religion of our fathers," would be no unprofitable ſpeculation. Accordingly, the ſplendid walks and fairy bowers of Idalia, which, till then, had only re-echoed the ſounds of gaiety and pleaſure, now reſounded with the vehement imprecations of
La

La Harpe againſt that vile revolutionary philoſophy of the Rights of Man, which had overthrown the religion of our fathers. Monſ. La Harpe continued to be the rage in Paris, till he was ſucceeded by another faſhionable novelty, which happened to be Abraham Effendi, the Turkiſh Ambaſſador. Upon Abraham Effendi's arrival, the faſhionable and butterfly-tribe forſook once more "the religion of their fathers," a fabric long ſince undermined, and now haſtening to decay, after gilding for a moment its venerable ruins with their glittering wings.

But another ſect was now ariſing, which threatened more formidable danger to the Roman Catholic religion than all the edicts of Jabobin ferocity. Some ſerious and well-intentioned men, who were ſenſible that the human mind without religion feels a void, which ſomething better muſt be found to fill

fill up than the doctrine of atoms, or the worship of reason, have become the founders of a new system, which, setting aside the dogmas of the Roman Catholic creed, connected, they assert, with ignorance and superstition, rests only on those points in which men of all religions are agreed, the moral goverment of the world by the Supreme Being, and the immortality of the soul. This sect, distinguished by the name of *Theophilanthropists,* the friends of God and man, had formed various little societies in Paris before their opinions were publicly known. The simplicity of their worship, somewhat resembling that of the Dissenters in England, gained the attention of a few lettered men, and the benevolence of their doctrines became the public theme of panegyric of a member of the Directory, Larevelliere Lepaux, who published a pamphlet, the object of which was to raise these doctrines into repute, by shewing the inconsistency fiftency of the Roman Catholic religion with liberty. This pamphlet was anfwered by Gregoire, the learned and patriotic Bifhop of Blois, with much warmth, as a calumny againft the nation : fince the great majority, he afferted, were both Catholics and Republicans, and the moft democratic governments in Europe, the fmaller Cantons of Switzerland, were ftedfaft in that belief.

La Revelliere Lepaux obtained the title of high-prieft of the new fect, which thus raifed into notice became the object of various calumnies. Some afferted it to be a neft of terrorifts, who, under the mafk of religion, and the liberty allowed to every kind of worfhip, met only to frame the means of bringing round again their late fyftem. Others were affured that this fect was nothing but a band of Atheifts and Philofophers, who affembled only to propagate principles which, difbelieving themfelves, selves, they intended to make inftruments of rooting out the Catholic faith.

Atheifts and Jacobins perhaps mingle in thefe congregations; but the mafs appears to be compofed of people of decent characters and manners, who, difcontented with their former creeds, have embraced this worfhip till they are provided with a better.

In their prayers they invoke the Supreme Being as the author and governor of the univerfe; they fing hymns of grateful acknowledgment for his bounties, and fill up the hours of their worfhip with a difcourfe on fome moral fubject, in which the obligations to maintain liberty, and keep inviolate the laws of the Republic are never forgotten. The better-informed among the Theophilanthropes are believers in Chriftanity, while others affect to talk with difdain of what they call the Chriftian fect: unwilling to admit, or probably ignorant that Chriftianity is the fole foundation on which refts their own fcanty belief.

This new religious fociety has the fupport of government in every way in which its influence can be directed, without infringing that impartiality in religious matters which the law requires. The modeft chambers, in which the founders of this fect firft affembled, are now changed for the fpacious churches which can fcarcely hold the crowds who refort to their meetings. The hour of the myfterious adoration of the hoft is no fooner paffed, than the affembly of the Theophilanthropes begin their fimple rites; and as the places of both worfhips are in common, the worfhippers of both opinions often mingle together and learn at leaft the divine leffon of toleration. How far the doctrines of this fociety may contribute

contribute to add to the stock of virtue in France it is difficult to determine; but this is certain, that the greatest revolutionary sinners, the Jacobins, have laid aside their worship of reason, and become the most stedfast adherents to this creed; and since the belief of immortality is the most powerful motive to virtue, he who is convinced of the existence of the Supreme Being, and offers up once a week his thanksgivings to the Giver of every good, for his loving-kindness and tender mercies, will be less inclined to sacrifice again at the altar of Moloch, and dye his hands in human blood.

The societies celebrate their worship both on Sundays and Decadies, in order to include the partisans of the old and new divisions of time. Their increasing numbers have compelled them to disseminate themselves in various quarters of the town, and they are about to apply for the equal use of all the churches of Paris, including that of Notre Dame. The people distinguish the two worships by the names of the mass and morality; and the new convert, instead of going as formerly *à la messe*, tells you, if you meet him on the way, that he is going *a la morale*.

CHAP. VI.

Country from Baſil to Zuric.—Bremgarton.—Balſtal.—Ornamented Graves.—French Burials.—Solemnity of Sunday in Switzerland.—Obſervations on Cruelty to Animals at Paris.—Geographical Religion of Suitzerland.

IN our route to Schaffhauſen we had paſſed the Haverſtein, a mountain which ſerves as a continuation of Mount Jura, and divides the Canton of Baſil from that of Soleure. On the top of this mountain, which is of difficult aſcent, we found a military poſt, where our permiſſions for travelling in Switzerland were examined and enregiſtered. This paſs is one of the keys of the country, and appears, from its ſituation, to be capable of being well defended againſt very ſuperior numbers; while the Canton of of Bafil, which lies at its bafe, has no natural fecurity whatever againft invafion.

The defcent from this mountain, through a paffage cut in the rock on its fummit, prefents many points of perfpective which we then thought fublime, for we had not yet gazed on thofe ftupendous monuments, before which all other objects fink into littlenefs.

From the town of Olten, belonging to the Canton of Soleure, and fituated at the diftance of half a league from the mountain, in a fine cultivated valley, through which flows the Aar; we proceeded along that river to Arau, in the Canton of Berne. A few miles beyond we croffed a river called the Da, at Lentzburg, a fmall neat town in the fame Canton; at Millingen we paffed the Reufs; this river, as well as the Limat, falls into the Aar, which, thus enriched by
the

the principal rivers of Switzerland, fvells to a mighty volume the waters of the Rhine.

The country from Olten to Schaffhaufen, though full of thofe beautiful landfcapes with which Switzerland abounds, prefents few fcenes except the noble views over the Lake of Zuric, which leave lafting traces on the memory.

On our return from Zuric we croffed a chain of hills on our left, and defcended into the rich vale of Bremgarten. Inftead of repaffing the Haverftein, we directed our courfe along the foot of Mount Jura, to meet the road that leads from Soleure over this ridge of mountains, which continues to feparate the two Cantons. At Balftal, a little village fituated at the foot of thofe mountains, we went to fee a cataract, of which we had heard a magnificent defcription.

tion. The rocky channel was bold and romantic, but the heat had dried up its waters. Our path lay through the churchyard of the village, and we were particularly ſtruck with the pious homage paid to the memory of the dead, not only in the gilded tomb-ſtones and painted croſſes, which were ſtuck thick over the ground; but in the humble affection which had given the grave itſelf an air of animation, by planting the pink, the violet, and other ſweet-ſcented herbs, on the green mounds, beneath which repoſed the mouldering duſt. Inſtead of the murky atmoſphere, and repulſive gloom of a receptacle of the dead, the church-yard, placed amidſt wooded rocks and paſtoral hills, and emitting the ſweet fragrance of newly-ſpringing flowers, and the freſh garlands which were hung around the tombs, excited pleaſing images of hope to the mind, and led to ſoothing meditation. I recollected the wiſh of Oſſian, fian, " O, lay me, ye that fee the light, near fome rock of my hills; let the thick hazels be around, let the ruftling oak be near. Green be the place of my reft; and let the found of the diftant torrent be heard."

How remote from thefe tender cares of mourning humanity is the treatment obferved in France towards the ead; and which might feem a relapfe to barbarifm, if we did not find, even among the moft favage nations, fome civilized marks of human reverence, fome decent ceremonial paid to the relicks of our mortal nature! It might, perhaps, be neceffary to reftrain the difplay of that vanity which, before the revolution, decked its mockery of woe with idle pomp and pageantry; but ftern indeed muft be the reformer, who admires that cold-blooded philofophy which configns thofe to whom we were bound by the holieft ties of humanity,

humanity, or the deareſt feelings of the heart, without regret, to the unhallowed proces-verbal of a municipal officer, who ſtrides away with indecent haſte before the yet unſtiffened corpſe, and, like death, the common leveller, hurls it into the common pit, among undiſtinguiſhed heaps of dead.

During the epocha of the worſhip of reaſon, a tacit approbation of this annihilation of vulgar prejudices might have been wrung from fear; ſince at that time, amongſt the well-fed monſters in the republic, death, and the grave—

—————— " Upturn'd
" Their noſtrils wide into the murky air,
" Sagacious of their quarry *—"

and revelled on the dead, as their pioneers, terror, and Jacobin-government, rioted on the living.

* Milton.

But

But when public or private fafety are no longer endangered by the indulgence of tender affections, even though equality fhould be fometimes wounded by the little diftinctions which they might love to confer on the mouldering clay, it is furely tyranny over the moft amiable weakneffes of our nature to tear thus rudely from the fond furvivor that form which, a few hours before, was folded to the heart in the laft agonies of feparation, and to which it ftill clings with the bitternefs of unavailing regret!

We returned to Bafil on a Sunday morning, time enough to join a throng of worfhippers at the French Proteftant church, whofe refpectful demeanour and devout attention formed a fingular and foothing contraft to the coarfe impiety we had fo lately witneffed at Paris; where we had feen
altars

altars overthrown, the surplice and the mitre transformed into caparisons for horses; had heard the commissaries of revolutionary committees boast, that at their Bacchanalian orgies their gross libations had been poured from sacramental cups, and had observed that no political blasphemy was so striking to those reformers as the slightest mark of respect for religion. The practice of shutting up the gates of the Swiss towns, during divine service, to prevent the rolling of carriages, though attended with inconvenience to travellers, is so far pleasing, as it consecrates one day in seven to relaxation and repose. The strict observance of this day of rest in Switzerland forms an agreeable contrast to the busy, as well as dissipated manner in which both Sunday and Decadi are passed in France; which festivals, being ever at war with each other, neither are celebrated with respect.

Not

Not only are the stated returns of intervals of rest necessary for man, but the voice of mercy calls aloud on the French legislature to interpose between the restless activity or avarice of the master, and the beast. Nothing is more pleasing than to observe throughout Switzerland the care, and even tenderness which is shewn to the animal creation; while in France they feel the primary curse of labour inflicted in all its severity. Sunday and Decadi, alike the loaded horse drags on his heavy burden; alike the merciless lash for ever resounds along the streets, and those whose nerves are not steeled against every pain but their own, are denied the relief of knowing, that an appointed respite from toil is the privilege of that miserable race.

Among the moral diversities of Switzerland, none are marked with more precision than

than their territorial belief. In a ride of two or three hours from the Canton of Bafil into that of Soleure, and over a branch of the Canton of Berne into that of Lucerne, we found ourfelves alternately on Catholic and Proteftant ground. In whatever caufe originated thefe whimfical boundaries of their geographical religion, which heretofore lighted up fo often the flames of civil diffention, it is foothing to obferve, that fince the beginning of the prefent century, the Swifs have difcovered that the fword is not the moft perfuafive weapon of religious controverfy. Two religions, that of the Roman church, and the affemblage of dogmas of the fixteenth century, called the Helvetic confeffion, are the exclufive religions of the Helvetic confederacy. Hume has fomewhere obferved, that the hatred of Polemics is moft inveterate, where the points in difpute are the leaft remote; it is not therefore

therefore furprifing that civil diffentions in Switzerland fhould have been carried to fuch excefs, fince the faith, for which both parties contended, is conceived in the fame fpirit of intolerance, and buried in the fame labyrinth of incomprehenfibility.

CHAP. VII.

Canton of Bafil.—Rights of the Burghers of Bafil.— Degraded State of the other Claffes.—Peafants.— Serfs.—Comparative View of French and Swifs Peafantry before the Revolution.—State of French Peafantry fince the Revolution.—Manufactures in the Canton of Bafil.—Singular Reftrictions on the Laborious Claffes.—Jews.—Citzens in France.—Toleration.—Defence of the Jews by a French Catholic Bifhop.—Religious Toleration in Turkey.—Whimfical Perfecution of the Jews at Bafil.—Reflections and Apoftrophe of a Jew.

OF the forty thoufand inhabitants, which compofe the population of the city and Canton of Bafil, the burghers forming the fifth part of that number alone enjoy, or fancy they enjoy the rights of equality. The people of Bafil are divided into two diftinct claffes, that of the burghers, confifting of eight thoufand perfons, and that of the other inhabitants; which laft clafs in-
creafes

creafes in the fame proportion that the firſt diminiſhes from year to year, and now amounts to about feven thoufand perfons. This latter clafs is in a ſtate of complete degradation, excluded from all political rights, can exercife no trade, and the individuals of which it is formed are confidered merely as ſtrangers, to whom the privilege is granted of living in the town, placed, for the moſt part, under the immediate refponfibility of the manufacturer or artizan by whom they are employed, and who is bound to take fuch meafures refpecting them, as fhall prevent their becoming burdenfome to the ſtate.

When perfons of this clafs are born in Bafil, when even their parents have been natives of the city for feveral fucceffive generations, they acquire not one further prerogative from thefe circumſtances; and the admiffion of a few of thefe individuals to the rights of burghers, is always attended with so many obstacles, that the instances in which it takes place are extremely rare. Few of this class attain considerable wealth, yet the increase of their number, their perseverance in remaining in this humiliating condition, while they are forced to support the load of heavy taxes from which the burghers are exempted, and receive no other benefit from the government than personal protection and safety, prove, however, that they at least enjoy some advantages of which they were not before possessed, and give a strong idea of the wretchedness of their situation in the countries which they have forsaken.

What is remarkable enough in this celebrated land of freedom, where the the poet tells us, that

" Even the peasant boasts his rights to scan,
" And learns to venerate himself as man:"

All

All the peasantry in the Canton of Basil, with only the exception of the little town of Liestal, which enjoys a few municipal privileges, are literally serfs, and annexed to the soil. In the feudal times, these people, who belonged to their respective chiefs, were successively sold, with the possessions on which they were found, to the city of Basil, then an imperial city. These Gothic prerogatives, however, have long since been prudently thrown into the back-ground, and are now less likely than ever to be revived, at the distance of half a mile from the shouts of equality, fraternity, and the rights of man.

A stranger who travels through France into Switzerland, cannot fail to observe the different appearance of the habitations of the peasantry of each country. The abject condition of this class in France, previous to the revolution, was one of the moſt prominent features of the wretchedneſs of the government; and ſufficient time has not yet elapſed to change the external marks of miſery. The commanding chateau ſtill frowns in gloomy magnificence, over the mud-walled hut, though the inhabitants are now poſſeſſed of equal rights. In Switzerland, the peaſant's habitation, however poor, has the air of comfort and convenience. Every wooden cottage has its garden, or orchard, and the limpid brook running before the door of the thatch, gives the whole an air of freſhneſs.

The peaſants of the Canton of Baſil are, like the generality of peaſants in Switzerland, well clothed and fed, have the liberty, which is no ſmall prerogative, of judging, in the firſt inſtance, their own diſputes, without the intervention of the Bailiff, whoſe

whose treasury is too often swelled by the fines of contention; and have also the privilege of bearing arms.

Their neighbours, the French peasantry, need no longer look upon these advantages with the glance of envy or the sigh of regret; since for the French husbandman, above every other class of Frenchmen, the revolution hitherto has been made. While the nobility, the clergy, the pensioners of the state, have been ruined; while commerce, for a while annihilated amidst the overwhelming shock of political convulsions, is now but slowly awakening once more to life, the husbandman, emancipated from every feudal claim, exonerated from every species of personal servitude, disburthened of every tax, and relieved from every oppression, has, above all others, had cause to bless the dawn of liberty. Even the horrible tempest of revolutionary terror

passed harmless over his head; and while the palace was devastated, and the chateau levelled to the ground, his cottage stood erect; amidst the violation of all other possessions, his property, with the exception of a few revolutionary requisitions, was respected; and, amidst hosts of executioners, his person was safe. During the long course and vast depreciation of paper-money, the farmer paid, with the labour of a week, the rents of the year; and was enabled, not only to augment his stock, but often became himself a purchaser of land. Sufficiently an egotist to take every possible advantage of circumstances, at the same time that he disbursed his rent in paper, he sold his corn only for money; while the starving proprietor of land, was compelled, like Belvidera, to " part with the antient ornaments of massy plate," to buy the wheat which grew on his own ground for the support of himself and his family. With the
return

return of money the landlord, indeed, has been refcued from poverty, by receiving his revenue in folid coin; which the farmers, immenfely enriched by the reign of paper, are well enabled to pay. They at prefent form a bold, independent clafs of yeomanry, a clafs till now unknown in this country, and their once bare-legged wives and daughters proudly difplay their white ftockings, rich-laced caps, fhining pendants, and golden croffes, which, in the country, ftill continue to be worn as a badge of their faith, as well as a decoration of their perfons.

The population of the Canton of Bafil being very far beyond the proportion of its extent of territory, great numbers are employed in manufactures, particularly that of cottons and ribbons, which are brought to great perfection. Over the manufacturers of thefe articles, the governors find it advantageous to manifeſt ſome portion of their right of ſovereignty; for in vain the father of a family may cultivate his field of flax, and prepare it for uſe; in vain his wife may ſpin, his infants turn the wheel which winds the thread, and he himſelf weave the woof; the web when woven is not at his diſpoſition—he has no right over the produce of his labour, no power to diſpoſe of what he has acquired by the ſweat of his brow and the toil of his hands; he muſt carry his little ſtock to the capital of his Canton, and there, and only there, is permitted to ſell it; while the burgher of the town, who is the purchaſer, has previouſly arranged the price at which it ſhall be ſold. A more vexatious law than this is, I believe, ſcarcely to be found in the whole code of deſpotiſm.

If ſuch be the paternal care of the political fathers of Baſil over their children, it would

would be superfluous to expect from them any marks of tender regard for those, who, as strangers, have no claim to their protection. But against none of the family of the human race is this republican choler so vehemently displayed, as against that miserable victim of Christian wrath and contempt, the follower of the religion of Moses. In despite of his imputed crimes, a dreadful legacy inherited from his ancestry, the Jew, who has found in many countries of Europe an asylum, in France has found a country. This despised wanderer can here cling fast to his home, and raised from that state of humiliation into which our Anti-Christian barbarity had plunged him, for ages the object of its severest persecution, the Jew, a citizen, becomes the proprietor of the soil, enriches himself in peace by the gains of his indusdustry, can lift his front in the senate, and become the highest officer in the state.

Divine

Divine fpirit of toleration! not of that toleration that throws the humiliating arm of protection over the creature of its forbearance, and, proud of its privileges, grants as a boon what ought to be conceded as a right; but of that toleration which regards as children of the fame original, and entitled to an equal fhare of his beneficence, the profeffors of the primitive faith of the Patriarchs, the followers of the dogmas of the Catholic creed, and of Calvin, and the believers in the fimple truths of the gofpel.

Againſt this innovating principle the Bafilians for two centuries paſt have ſtruggled with zealous uniformity. Previous to the French revolution, the epocha of Jewiſh liberty, Gregoire, diſtinguiſhed no lefs for a ſtrict adherence to his own faith, than for that large benevolence of foul which hails a brother in every religious creed, became the avowed advocate of this perfecuted race, and

and prepared their way to liberty, by inculcating on the minds of their perfecutors the heavenly leffon of toleration. Even the pale-faced crefcent, catching fome particles of its divine light, has at length reflected its favoring beams on the celebration of Chriftian worfhip. But in the Proteftant Canton of Bafil no Catholic rites are allowed, and a Jew is an object of unceafing abhorrence. Not only is the refidence of thefe elder brethren of their faith forbidden by the burghers of Bafil; but without the exprefs permiffion of the fupreme magiftrate, or hazarding the payment of a heavy fine, durft any Ifraelitifh wanderer reft within the walls for one night his wearied head. No act of commerce can pafs between a Jew and a Bafilian, however equal their talents in the arts of trade, without the intervention of a public officer in aid of the latter; and fo careful is the protecting hand of government in favor of the burgher, that no contract

contract with a Jew, unless ratified by the burgo-master, is binding on the believer.

It has been invidiously stated, that the jealousy of trade has suggested these prudent precautions; but the superior attainments of the inhabitants of Basil, in the science of commerce, renders such a precaution unnecessary. No person of discernment will put in competition the fine commercial intelligence of a burgher of Basil, with the rude cunning of the miserable outcast of his proscription; and this zeal against Judaism must be resolved into the abhorrence with which Basil Christians consider this impious sect, delivered over to final reprobation. The Jew, who does not understand the niceties of Basil belief, might indeed reasonably expect to find in a free state the privileges allowed to his brethren in despotic countries by Catholic inquisitors: he may perhaps be allowed

allowed to murmur at the detail of inhofpitality with which he is treated at Bafil, and exclaim with the Jew of Venice:

"O, Father Abraham, what thefe Chriftians are!"
SHAKESPEAR.

CHAP. VIII.

Government of the Canton of Basil.—Mode of Election of the Members of the Council, and of the Professors of the University.—Ancient and Modern State of Literature.

WHEN we observe in the Canton of Basil, which is composed of forty thousand inhabitants, that more than thirty thousand of that number enjoy no privileges, it will be some relief to find that liberty has taken refuge among the remainder. The actual number of burghers does not exceed seven thousand, and of these no more than three hundred wield the sceptre of government for life, under the name of members of the great and little councils.

Although, when vacancies take place, the members of these councils are chosen from amongst

amongſt the burghers, they are not choſen by them. The care of the nomination falls to the lot of the members of the councils themſelves, who, knowing from experience the fatigues and difficulties of governing, are ſuppoſed to be better informed than the maſs of the burghers, what heads are beſt organized for the duties of that important ſtation.

The right of citizenſhip is never acquired, as in France, by reſidence: the ambitious wight who aſpires to this diſtinction, after obtaining the permiſſion of the grand council, muſt purchaſe the privilege with a large ſum of money, unleſs he becomes enamoured of ſome fair daughter of a burgher, when he is allowed to make a compoſition for his freedom by paying one half in money, and as a compromiſe for the other, taxing himſelf with a wife. But though admitted to be a burgher, the privilege

lege of being eligible to any office of the government belongs only to his posterity of the third or fourth generation. Criminal conviction suspends all civil rights, and the crime of bankruptcy at Basil, ranked by other governments under the class of misfortunes, attaints with the same degradation even the highest officers of the state.

Lest thirty-nine thousand seven hundred inhabitants of the Canton of Basil should murmur at being governed by three hundred self-elected individuals, means have been taken to lessen the appearance of this usurpation in the eyes of the people. With this view the elections of the vacant seats of government are made by lot: when a vacancy happens six candidates are chosen by the great council, after which those candidates draw lots for the place.

This mode of election may perhaps be pardonable

pardonable with refpect to the members of the great and little council. Perhaps no eminent talents are requifite to fill thofe ftations, or to perform the parts of burgo-mafters or tribunes; and indeed the opinion, that it requires little art to govern, appears to be fpreading fo generally throughout Europe, that in many parts of it men feem difpofed to govern themfelves.

But what is not to be forgiven is having adopted this mode of drawing lots to fill up the vacant feats at the univerfity. Thofe fuperior endowments of mind, which give the right of prefiding over the refearches of fcience, are in all ages and nations difpenfed with parfimony, and at Bafil are probably for the moft part difpenfed in vain: fince no doubt chance often bids dullnefs mount the throne, while black-balled genius " waftes its talents on the defart air." Of this there is a remarkable inftance on the records

records of the university, where those ornaments of their country, the illustrious mathematicians, the Bernouillis, who would have been the ornaments of any country, after frequent rejection by black-balls, obtained at length the chairs of professors of rhetoric and botany.

It may indeed be now alledged in justification of this practice, that there is little to teach since there are few to learn: the colleges are without pupils, and the professorships are merely sinecures. Yet Basil was once the centre of science, the chosen residence of the great Erasmus, and possessed an university, the professors of which were composed of the most enlightened men of the age, and on which the Eulers, and the Boehmens conferred celebrity: and we are told by Mr. Cox, that he found shopkeepers in this city reading Virgil, Horace, and Plutarch; from which he was, no doubt,

doubt, well authorized to draw his conclufion, that there is no country in the world where the people are fo happy. But whatever were the Halcyon days of tafte and learning at the period of Mr. Cox's vifit, it is a melancholy fact, that this literary fpirit has entirely evaporated fince his departure. Thefe lettered triumphs, the " tales of other times," are buried in tenfold gloom: the Swifs themfelves admit, that Bafil is the Bœotia of their country, and Horace, Virgil, and Plutarch, are now in general difrepute, not only among the fhopkeepers, but even among the wholefale dealers of this once claffic city.

Science is in few countries the certain road to wealth, but the modern rulers of Bafil feem to have determined, that it fhall there be the fure path to poverty. Since, while thofe citizens, whofe knowledge extends only to the rules of arthmetic, who

read nothing but their ledgers, and understand nothing but the courfe of exchange,
enjoy all the lavifh luxuries of affluence,
the ill-fated wight whom the love of learning, or the impulfe of genius leads to the
profefforfhip of a college, is forced to content himfelf with that narrow ftipend,
which, inftead of keeping pace with the
increafe of wealth, remains, amidft its flowing tide, an antique monument of the few
and fimple wants of early times.

But to have annexed poverty to letters
appears not to have been thought fufficient
by that portion of the praife-worthy Helvetic body, which prefides over the deftinies
of Bafil. They have ftamped a mark of
difgrace on the brow of fcience; and whilft
the taylor, the fifherman, the fhoe-maker,
the boatman, all men but the man of letters, can affert their claims as burghers to
the public honors and dignities of the ftate,

" And

"And faving ignorance enthrones by law;"
                                    POPE.

the profeffors of the univerfity are excluded. Genius is treated like other ftrangers in the city of Bafil, and refufed all participation in the rights and immunities of its privileged burghers.

Even here, however, we find a chofen few have not bowed the knee to Baal, and who cultivate letters with the ardor of elegant minds; but their number is not fufficient to fave their city from reproach, and thofe accomplifhed exceptions only ferve to eftablifh the general rule, as a folitary flower on a defart heath reminds the traveller of the furrounding barrennefs. While I recall the few men of fuperior intellectual endowments, which Bafil ftill can boaft, the image of my venerable friend, Colonel Frey, naturally prefents itfelf to my mind: that refpectable veteran in literature as well as arms, who unites with thofe polifhed manners, acquired during fifty years of military fervice in France, all the more folid attainments of learning and fcience: he poffeffes a fine library, one of the few cabinets of natural hiftory at Bafil, which, rich in petrifications, marbles, and minerals, deferves the attention of ftrangers, and paffes the evening of an active life in the placid fatisfactions of ftudy. I enjoyed the advantage of his protection during my ftay at Bafil, and have a fufficiently difcerning fenfe of merit to know how to appreciate his friendfhip. Colonel Frey's fecond fon is married to M. du F———, the romantic hiftory of whofe parents is fketched in my firft volume of letters on France.

Mr. Le Grand, member of the great council, an ardent and enlightened friend of the French Republic, had taught his infants to lifp the cherifhed founds of liberty, and chaunt its favorite airs with such fond enthusiasm, that his house seemed to me a chapel worthy of William Tell.

Although the number of enlightened men in Basil is very inconsiderable, it is easy to perceive, that in the general resurrection to liberty, which Switzerland is about to experience, this Canton, to borrow an expression from Gibbon, will, from its moral and geographical position, be the first to cast away the shroud.

CHAP. IX.

Curiosities of Basil.—Arsenal.—Cathedral.—Public Library.—Dance of Death.—Departure from Basil.—Sempack.—Reflections on the Love of Freedom.

During our stay at Basil, we visited, like other travellers, the arsenal, the ornaments of which are composed of shields, swords, and breast-plates, which, from their enormous size, would crush ten modern citizens of Basil, and reminded us of Nestor's speech, where he exclaims—

" A god-like race of heroes once I knew,
" Such as no more these aged eyes shall view."
Pope's Homer.

We then proceeded to the cathedral, a fine piece of architecture, but disfigured without by a coating of red paint: what is most interesting within is the tomb of Erasmus,

Erasmus, a frugal tablet of common marble stuck against the wall.

At the public library we were shewn, with extreme politeness, the various and valuable curiosities it contains; such as the collection of manuscripts which is highly precious, manuscript letters of Erasmus, the original sketches of most of the fine pictures of Holbein, the Passion painted in the first style of this master, and other admirable pieces worthy of the public library and museum of Paris.

We saw M. Mechel's fine collection of engravings, and we also visited the hideous series of figures called the Dance of Death, and painted by Kleber, a pupil of Holbein. After seeing these, and some other less important curiosities, we took leave of our friends at Basil, in order to enjoy a nearer view of those sublime objects, which we had

had hitherto seen only at a distance, lifting their hoary heads to the heavens.

We crossed again the Haverstein, and passed through Olten to Arbourg, a small town on the river Aar, overlooked by a castle, which is the northern bastile of the Canton of Berne for state-offenders. From Zoffingen, a pleasant and populous town about two leagues from Arbourg, we proceeded through a delicious country of gently swelling hills, and finely watered meadows, to Surfee, a town of the Canton of Lucerne. Half a mile from Surfee is the Lake of Sempach, along which we travelled nearly the whole of its length, and which takes its name from a little town on the eastern side, where was fought that ever memorable battle which gave liberty to Switzerland. With equal contempt of their numbers and discipline, Duke Leopold, at the head of a formidable phalanx, and attended

tended by the firft nobility of the empire attacked the little army, confifting of thirteen hundred men of the four confederate Cantons, Lucerne, Uri, Schweitz, and Underwalden. The Swifs had in vain attempted to pierce the enemy's ranks, and the fate of war hung doubtful; when Arnold de Wilkenreid, devoting himfelf, like Decius, to certain death, after recommending his wife and children to the care of his country, opened the way to victory, by throwing himfelf on the lances of the Auftrians, who, feized with aftonifhment at this effort of defperate valour, yielded to the impetuous torrent for which Wilkenreid had freed a paffage, and fled; leaving Leopold on the field with the flower of his army.

On the fpot where this memorable victory was gained, is built a chapel in commemoration of the event; in which are feen the portraits of the Duke of Auftria and

and his chief nobility who perifhed with him, and whofe bodies were tranfported for burial to fome diftant abbey, while the afhes of the Swifs heroes yet confecrate the field of honor where they fo generoufly poured out their lives. Several of thefe chapels, the monuments of the piety and valour of the early Swifs, are to be feen in this country. As feftivals and games were inftituted among the Greeks to keep alive the heroical deeds of their anceftors, fo the Swifs, on the anniverfary of great events, were accuftomed to go in folemn proceffion to thofe chapels, and offer up their public thanfgivings.

This practice, which has been long difcontinued in other parts of Switzerland, is ftill obferved at this chapel. Every year, on the ninth of July, a folemn mafs is performed, and an oration fuitable to the occafion is pronounced; the Republic of Lucerne

Lucerne defrays the expence, and some of the magistates attend the service. The inhabitants of this district are not altogether unconscious that they live in the neighbourhood of heroes. The person who undertook to be our Cicerone, was a smart-looking hostess of a village inn.—" There," said she, " on the brow of that hill we stood, dressed in carters' frocks, and the Austrians thought we were a fresh army of soldiers." By *we* were meant the women of that day, who, according to local tradition, for it does not appear to be recorded in any history, made use of this stratagem to multiply the appearance of the confederated forces. Had our Cicerone lived at that period, there is no doubt, from the energy with which she imputed to herself the feats of her ancestry, that she would have been foremost in the van of this *corps de reserve*.

The remembrance of the illustrious acts of

of their anceftors is cherifhed by enflaved nations with fond enthufiafm, and even degenerated nations attempt to hide their own difgrace beneath the glories of their hiftory. When the French armies lately entered Greece, the Patriarch, at the head of the proceffion, met the conquerors with the books of Homer. Though bowed beneath the yoke of European tyranny,

> " Th' unconquerable mind, and freedom's holy flame,"

Is felt not only by

> ———— " the favage youth
> " Beneath the odorous fhade
> " Of Chili's boundlefs forefts laid;"
>
> GRAY.

but throughout the immenfe tract of that rich and violated continent, where the Peruvian, ftealing from the glance of his tyrant, hies to the native circle, joins in the melancholy dance, and laments, with tears,

tears, the departed splendour of his country*.

* Of the existence of this fond enthusiasm I have lately heard much from some well informed Frenchmen, who had been long resident in that part of the globe, and who, under the false pretence of their being engaged in a conspiracy in favor of liberty, were thrown into the dungeons of Mexico, where they remained loaded with irons till after the conclusion of the peace between France and Spain, when they were ordered to leave the country. The Viceroy of Mexico, brother of the Prince de Paix, as a reward for his vigilant persecution of those French citizens, was decorated by his Court with the title of Reconquistador, and a second Cortez.

When in my poem on Peru, one of my earliest productions, I fondly poured forth the wish that the natives of that once happy country might regain their freedom, it seemed rather the illusive dream of fancy than founded on any solid basis of hope. That revolution had not yet taken place, which appears destined to break the fetters of mankind in whatever region they are found, and which transforms what was once the vision of poetic enthusiasm into the sober certainty of expectation.

The

The human mind, frozen under the superstition of ages, unfolds itself to the genial gale of freedom, passing even for a moment over its stiffened faculties. The transient revolt of Rhenzi was regarded by Petrarch as the return of the golden age of Rome; and the subject of the Italian Pontiff views, at the present day, the light of freedom reflected from the rocks of the Cisalpine Republic on the capitol, and hails the happy augur.

Festivals in favour of liberty, had they been habitual in Switzerland, would probably have been forbidden by the policy of the times. It would have been dangerous to have kindled fuel near so mighty a conflagration. But where the spirit of liberty is to be preserved or excited, as in France, perhaps no means is more effectual than that of the periodical commemoration of great events.

events. What Frenchman can hear, unmoved, the names of Fleurus, Lodi, Kell, Arcole, and the Tagliamento?—but were the long lift of French victories to be commemorated, the calendar itfelf would fcarcely contain the catalogue.

CHAP. X.

Lucerne.—Voyage down the Lake of Lucerne.—Gerfau.—Schweitz.—Brunnen.—Tell's Chapel.—Lake of Uri.

AFTER leaving the lake of Sempach, we ascended the hills that lead to Lucerne. From their summits, we were first presented with the near view of that grand and majestic scenery, which we had hitherto only beheld at a distance. Mount Pilate, lifted high above the rolling clouds its shagged head; of which, at intervals, we caught a glance, while its dark green sides contrasted finely with the varied vegetation around us.

The approach to Lucerne is beautifully picturesque. About half a league from the town

town we crossed the Emmen, near the spot where it mingles its streams with the Reuss, which pours its swelling and limpid waters of a grassy hue from the lake. Lucerne is divided by this river, and the lake, into unequal portions, but the communication is rendered easy and agreeable by means of four bridges; one of which of ordinary construction, serves for the passage of carriages, while the other three are calculated only for foot passengers. These bridges, one of which is six or seven hundred feet in length, and another from three to four hundred feet, present delightful views over the lake to the mountains, and serve as walks to the inhabitants, who are sheltered from the sun and rain, by a roof supported at every ten steps by pillars of wood: between those pillars pannels are fixed, painted on both sides, which represent in some places the most celebrated events of their national history, and in others scripture-fubjects, and fanciful figures of poetry and romance, fuch as winged dragons, griffins, devils, and centaurs:

"Monfters and Hydras, and Chimæras dire."
MILTON.

Some of thefe paintings are well executed; but are unfavorably placed on account of the fhadow of the roof. One of our Lucerne friends pointed out a piece which reprefented an execution, the inftrument of death refembles the machine, of which fuch abhorred ufe was made in France during the reign of terror, and robs of the merit of the invention a member of the firft national affembly, M. Guillotin, whofe name it bears.

As we wifhed to crofs the Alps without delay, we remained but a fhort time at Lucerne, intending on our return to take a more detailed view of this enchanting country.

country. Before our departure we made a visit to General Pfyffer, whose plan in relief of the little Cantons is an interesting monument of topographical genius and laborious constancy. The General related to us with his usual affability, all the perils and difficulties he had encountered in the formation of this admirable mimick-creation of silver torrents, mossy forests, tin houses, and glass lakes.

We embarked our horses, and departing from Lucerne at an early hour of a fine cloudless morning, began our voyage down the lake to Altorf. The hills rising from the shores near the town, which are but of little elevation, are covered for the most part with country-houses and gardens; and here the inhabitants, instead of warring with nature by strait lines and trimmed trees, had aided her loveliness by their taste in disposition and forbearance in ornament.

At the diftance of three miles from Lucerne the lake opens on both fides, ftretching away on the left to the Canton of Zug, and on the right to that of Underwalden. On the one fide Mount Pilate, rifing abrupt from the waters, difplayed its fublime and uncovered head: on the other the lofty but more humble Rigi poured down its numerous torrents, illuminated by the funbeams, like filvered lines in fwift fucceffion, at which we gazed with delight, while we were paffing along tremendous rocks, whofe vaft fhadows fell black upon the clear azure of the waters. Before us the mountains fwelled majeftically, clothed with a luxuriancy of trees; but as we proceeded the rocks narrowed, and feemed to forbid our progrefs.

At this point the breadth of the lake is very inconfiderable; but having paffed thefe ftraights a turn of the rock difcovers another

ther ample sea, whence we discerned the lofty hills of Uri on our right; and to the west a considerable portion of the refluent lake that washed the rocks of Underwalden.

On the left, beneath the inaccessible and encircling craggs of the Rigi, is situated the independent state of Gersau, where we disembarked.

This Republic comprehending its regency, single, double, and triple councils, treasurer, grand sautier, secretaries, judges, ministers, officers, naval and military force, and the governed of all descriptions, contains from nine hundred to a thousand souls. Cavalry makes no part of the strength of this territory, since the lofty ramparts of rock, by which it is divided from the main land, are inaccessible to horses. It possesses, however, a numerous fleet of boats, which

rode

rode at anchor before the port, and prevented for some time the entrance of our vessel. Having on our landing sauntered to one part of the state to take a survey of its edifices, our ears were assailed by a tumultuous noise, which proceeded from the tuneful throats of a multitude assembled in the church at the other end of the republic, celebrating the praises of Saints Zeno and Bridget.

The chief import of this republic is raw silk, which is manufactured for Basil and Zurich; its exports are principally fruit and fish, in the capture of which the fleet is employed which we saw moored in the harbour.

Gersau allied itself to the Democratic Cantons in the beginning of the fourteenth century, and adopted their form of government. The history of the wars and treaties, troubles

troubles, domestic and foreign, of this small republic, though it make no considerable figure in the history of the world, fills many a page in the records of the Lake of the four Cantons.

The earliest warlike atchievement of Gersau appears to have been directed against Lucerne. Discontented with a decision given by the Canton of Zug, as arbitrator, in favour of the Lucernois, the Gersovians, like Homer's heroes, began hostilities by stealing the cattle of their neighbours of Wigis,

"When from their fury fled the trembling swains,
"And theirs was all the plunder of the plains;
"Fifty white flocks, full fifty herds of swine,
"As many goats, as many lowing kine."

POPE's ILIAD, Book xi.

Reprisals were made, and the contest might perhaps have been as bloody as that of the Pylian

Pylian Sage with the Epian powers, had not the allied Cantons interfered, and imposed a heavy retribution on the Gersovians.

This republic, which is said to be the least in Switzerland, and perhaps in Europe, and is scarcely known beyond the ken of the craggs, and the lake that surround it, far from furnishing us with new themes of the happiness and security of such humble states, bore many marks of the vices and defects of more extensive governments. A few handsome mansions, surrounded by wretched cabins, and infested by beggars, afforded no presumptive evidence of an equal distribution of power or wealth. The republic of Gersau, however, has sometimes had the honour of holding the balance of Swiss power, and is said at the famous battle of Cappel, in which Zuinglius fell, to have turned the scale in favour of of the caufe for which they fought, and to have been one of the principal inftruments in the prefervation of the Catholic Religion in Switzerland.

After having vifited whatever was worthy of notice at Gerfau, we reimbarked and proceeded on our voyage. The Canton of Schweitz lay in the direction we were failing, prefenting us with a fine perfpective of woody and romantic country, rifing from floping hills, on the fide of which the town of Schweitz is built, into lofty forefts of pines, which are crowned by two towering mountains with fharp pointed peaks. The town of Brunnen is the port of this Canton, and the road from thence to Schweitz, about two miles diftance, is an agreeable walk, which is ufually taken by every traveller who fails up this lake; fince few refufe to turn a little out of their way in order to tread upon the spot which gives its name to Switzerland.

The shores of the Lake of the four Cantons have witnessed most of the great actions that have been performed in Switzerland; as those of the Mediterranean have been the scenes of whatever has most dignified the history of the world. At Brunen, in 1315, the treaty was confirmed between the countries of Uri, Schweitz, and Underwalden, which asserted their independence. At Grutlen, a village at the foot of the Seelisburg, on the opposite side of the lake, was held the confederacy where the generous design was planned by the three heroes for the deliverance of their country. The chapel of William Tell, as we advanced, presents itself on the right, perched among the rocks, in commemoration of his escape from the bailiff Geisler, by leaping from
the

the boat in the midſt of a tempeſt raiſed by ſubterraneous winds, which often render this navigation dangerous.

No place could ſurely be found more correſpondent to a great and generous purpoſe, more worthy of an heroical and ſublime action, than the auguſt and ſolemn ſcenery around us. The Lake which we had traverſed nearly from weſt to caſt, turns direct from the point oppoſite Brunen to the ſouth, and is ſaid to be in this part ſix or ſeven hundred feet deep. This branch is called the Lake of Uri. Near its entrance inſulated pointed rocks of ſingular form and conſtruction riſe boldly from the water. Having paſſed thoſe precipices, we entered into a gulph, of which the boundaries were awfully terrific. On each ſide of the profound abyſs, the dark lowering rocks roſe ſometimes abrupt, and barren, ſometimes preſenting tufts of pine and beech

beech between its fhaggy maffes, and occafionally beyond thefe favage limits of the lake, the eye caught a glimpfe of mountains in the lofty perfpective, clothed midway with forefts, and rifing into peaks of alternate pafturage and craggs.

Beneath their inacceffible ramparts, whofe enormous height gives an appearance of narrownefs to the lake, we failed, gazing with that kind of rapt aftonifhment which fears to difturb, or be difturbed by the mutual communication of thought. The approach of night fpread new forms of fhadowy greatnefs over the fcene. We had loitered many hours on our paffage, forgetting that the laft part of our voyage was the moft perilous. But the unruffled ftillnefs of the water, the delicious ferenity of the evening, and the long reflected rays of the moon from the whitened fummits of the oppofite mountains, of which we fometimes
caught

caught a glimpse, diffipated every idea of danger. The only founds that broke the awful filence were the gentle motion of the oars of our wearied boatmen, and the tolling of the diftant bell from Altorf, borne down the lake, and

" Swinging flow with fullen roar."
MILTON.

We had paffed through all the foft gradations of twilight, and had enjoyed the browneft horrors of evening in all their deepening gloom, before the moon had fcaled the lofty fummits which concealed her from our view. At length fhe burft upon us in her fulleft radiancy, illumining the dufky fides of the cragged rocks, and the dark foliage of the piny woods; burnifhing with her filver rays the fmooth and limpid waters; fhooting her fhadowy beams along the lake to the diftant perfpective

tive of the mountains we had left behind; and lighting up the whole majeſtic ſcenery with glorious and chaſtened luſtre.

We reached almoſt with regret Fluellen, the port whither we were bound, and mounting our horſes proceeded to Altorf, which lies at the diſtance of two miles.

CHAP. XI.

Altorf.—William Tell.—Ascent to St. Gothard.—Waffen.—Valley of Schellinen.—Devil's Bridge.—Vale of Urseren.

NOTWITHSTANDING our impatience to climb St. Gothard, it would have been unpardonable not to have passed a few hours in contemplating the most remarkable objects at Altorf, the capital of Uri, and the laurelled cradle of the Helvetic confederation.

Two hundred years since, the tree yet stood erect in the market-place, to which the son of William Tell was bound. On this sacred spot is built a kind of painted tower, and at some little distance, where it is said the father stood, when he shot the apple from his son's head, a public foun-

tain is erected, called Tell's fountain; on which is placed the frowning statue of this generous deliverer of his country. There must surely be some defect in the heart, which feels no enthusiastic glow, while we tread over the spots where those heroes have trod, who have struggled for the liberties of mankind, or bled for their rights. Yet one of that everlasting race of doubters, who wage an eternal war with all those sublime traditions, those heroical sacrifices, and those deeds of greatness, which it is delightful to believe, has destroyed with a touch of his sterile pen all the bright images with which imagination peoples this scene of marvels, by asserting in a treatise, published thirty years since at Berne, that all the romantic feats of William Tell were in far remoter times performed by Toko, a Dane, against Harold, a king of Denmark, in the tenth century. This cold inquirer was probably not aware of all the disagreeable

able senfations, which would be felt by enthusiastic travellers, who had been worshipping the statue of Tell, when they were informed that their homage should be addressed to Toko. It is indeed pretended that there is an unfortunate co-incidence of circumstances in the narration of the Danish historian, with respect to the shooting at the apple, and the speech made to the tyrant. The sovereign council of Berne, however, ordered the book to be burnt, and I feel much inclined to excuse this coercive measure of those puissant Lords, since I cannot but share their resentment. Tell is in England, as well as Switzerland, the hero of our infancy; the marvellous tale of the apple is one of our earliest lessons, and who can endure to give to Toko those trophies, which he has been taught from childhood were the rights of Tell! The only circumstance in the Saxon's favor, or rather that of the author who cites him; is the modesty

desty with which he delivers his doubts: had he lived in our days, he would, perhaps, have allegorized William Tell and Toko himself, with as little ceremony as M. Dupuis, and his less learned pupils in infidelity, have allegorized the most sacred characters of antiquity. The fantastic speculations of these later Pyrrhonists have indeed been treated with more severity than the fable of the Historian. The political infallibility of a sovereign council may perhaps be arraigned, and Rousseau suggests, " that burning is not answering;" but who shall raise up the whimsical tribe of Allegorists, crushed beneath the logical wit of the philosophical believer?

After leaving Altorf, we journeyed along a valley of three leagues, through which the Reuss flows with the ordinary rapidity of a Swiss river.

About

About six miles from Altorf, we passed by a chapel in a meadow; the façade of which was decorated with a highly coloured painting, representing a stag-hunt, which appeared to be a singular ornament for a place of religious worship. We found upon inquiry, that this meadow was one of the places of general assembly, that it was called the Jag-Matt, or hunting meadow; and that on the day of St. Mark the whole country march to this chapel in procession.

The rocks, clothed at intervals with trees of various sorts rose high and steep on each side of the valley, which wore a fertile and smiling appearance till we came to the village of Stag; above which the Alps first lift their majestic heads. Here we began to ascend that mass of mountains, which is rather the base than the mountain itself of St. Gothard. The road suddenly becomes so steep,

steep, that it required at first some address to keep a seat on horseback. The river, which glided gently through the valley on its expanded bed, being now hemmed in by rocks, begins to struggle for its passage at a profound depth. The pine clad-hills rose on each side to our farthest ken, down which torrent streams were rushing, and crossed our way to mingle themselves with the Reuss, which continually presented new scenes of wonder. The mountains seemed to close upon us as we advanced, sometimes but just space enough was left to admit the passage of the river foaming through the rocks, which seem obstinately to oppose its passage. The road lay for a considerable length on the left side of the precipices, from which we beheld the struggles of the waters, and the tremendous succession of cascades which they formed. An abrupt precipice, forbidding the continuance of the road on this side, a bridge of hardy construction

tion led to the oppofite mountain, which is afcended, till meeting with a fimilar obftruction, we croffed the ftream again to the left.

On one of thefe bridges, we halted to gaze upon the fcene around us, and the yawning gulph below. The depth is fo tremendous, that the firft emotion, in looking over the bridge is that of terror, left the fide fhould fall away and plunge you into the dark abyfs; and it requires fome reflection to calm the painful turbulence of furprize, and leave the mind the full indulgence of the fenfations of folemn enthufiaftic delight, which fwell the heart, while we contemplate fuch ftupendous objects.

The name of this bridge, in the language of the country, is the Prieft's leap; whether the holy man leapt over the gulph, or into it, is not remembered, but it is difficult to hear the ſtory on the ſpot without an involuntary ſhudder, or fancy yourſelf in perfect ſecurity.

> " The very place puts toys of deſperation,
> " Without more motive into every brain,
> " That looks ſo many fathoms to the gulph,
> " And hears it roar beneath."
>
> SHAKESPEARE.

The road up to the village of Waſſen is highly romantic: here the induſtry of men has tamed ſome of thoſe wild torrents, of which ſuch numbers run idly to waſte; and ſawing mills and other machinery owe their impulſe to thoſe ſwiftly deſcending volumes. In this village we halted to repoſe from our fatigues, and began to feel ſome of the mountain breezes which contraſted very agreeably with the concentrated heat that had ſubdued us in the valley beneath. It was Sunday, the day was fine, and the village was crouded with the mountaineers

taineers who had come in to keep the festival, and practife, as they do every week in some village of the Canton, the art of shooting at a mark, which, independent of the amusement, is a duty imposed on every citizen, who, under the inspection of a magistrate, is obliged in the course of the year to fire a certain number of rounds, that he may keep his arms in order, and not forget the means of defending his country in case of invasion. We could yet see no traces of snow, except in the numerous torrents which rolled down the enormous mountains, the streams of which were considerably increased from a cause that in less mountainous countries would have produced an opposite effect, the excessive heat and dryness of the weather, which melted the snows of the Glaciers.

The views around Waffen are astonishing for their variety as well as beauty. You perceive,

perceive, however, after paſſing the village, that you are advancing into a country where man is obliged to be continually at war with nature. On one ſide the mountain was ſtripped of its piny clothing to ſome extent, diſcovering, inſtead of dark green foliage, a bare rocky and gravelly waſte, interſperſed with wrecks of trees. This, we were told, was the ravage of an avalanche. When whole foreſts of majeſtic height are ſwept away with irreſiſtible fury, what means of defence can human force oppoſe to ſuch mighty deſtruction? Men, however, live tranquilly amidſt the danger, and build their houſes in ſuch poſitions, and after ſuch a conſtruction, that the enemy, even if he chances to take the direction of their habitations, may paſs over them unhurt.

Roeks, for the moſt part, are made their allies againſt theſe invaſions from the ſnowy moun-

mountains; but even rocks, coeval with time, often yield to the terrible devaftation. As we advanced, the country, which had hitherto prefented fcenes of blended grace and majefty, began to affume an afpect of favage wildnefs and terror. A few habitations and green fpots amidft thefe deferts, gave ftill fome relief to the piece; but after paffing the little village of Geftinen, and the torrent of the Meyen which croffes the road to increafe the waters of the Reufs, all is tremendous and awful. Here no pines wave their lofty heads, no mountain fhrubs difplay their fimple flowrets, nor does even a blade of weed betray the poffibility of exiftence to any thing that breathes.

It was now the moft luxuriant part of fummer; we had left the glowing harvefts beneath ripe for the fickle, and the fruits at two or three leagues diftance hung in lavifh clufters upon the bough; but in this region

region it not only was winter, but a winter that seemed here to have fixed its eternal abode; for not only were there no traces of renovation to inspire hope, but the impossibility of change was every where obdurately marked. Immense piles of naked rock, not less lofty than the mountains along which we passed, rose sometimes perpendicularly above our heads, and sometimes falling back, left between the road and their horrid tops immense masses that seemed shivered from their sides, forming vast fields of rock.

This passage, which in summer is sufficiently terrific, becomes dangerous in winter by the frequent avalanches that rush from those tremendous heights, and so delicately are these messengers of destruction hung on the summits, that the guides and mule-drivers tye up the bells of their cattle to prevent the gingling, and forbid a word
to

to be spoken by the paffengers, that the avalanche, which waits on the mountain to overwhelm them, may not hear them approach. Little croffes placed by the road fide where travellers have perifhed, are melancholy mementos of fuch mortal accidents, againſt which, however, precautions are taken, by firing mufkets to fhake the air and precipitate the impending avalanche. Huge fragments of rocks fometimes prefent themfelves as if they threatened to obftruct the way; and we remarked one enormous piece of beautiful granite that fkirted the road, and is called the devil's ftone, which, on account of fome mifunderftanding with the people of the country, he brought down from the mountain to deftroy fome of the works he had himfelf formerly conftructed.

If any fuperſtition is pardonable, it is that of the inhabitants of this mountain, and

and had the epic poets from Homer, down to our sublime Milton, seen this valley of Schellinen before they described their Tartarus or Pandemonium, they would have caught some new images of the savage and terrific, and their hells would have been habitations less desirable.

The devil of this country, however, cannot, in the estimation of the rude mountaineers, be the same malignant mischievous fiend which the inhabitants of plains and civilized countries make him, since, if he has chosen this chaos of nature for his habitation, he has not shut up his palace, like other stately monarchs, from the vulgar eye, but, on the contrary, has unfolded the recesses of his dwelling by opening ways, and building bridges, which the mountaineers believe none but himself could have constructed, and by which he has certainly " deserved well of the country."

Nothing

Nothing can be imagined more bold and daring than the road that leads through the valley of Schellenen to the mountain of St. Gothard; the difficulties appear almoſt inſurmountable; ſometimes the road ſeems ſo narrow between frightful precipices on each ſide, that great blocks of granite are placed on the edges as ſafeguards to the paſſengers; and where the mountain forbids all poſſibility of paſſage, offering an impenetrable rampart by its vertical abruptneſs, the path juts out from the ſide ſupported by arches and pillars, which are built up from ſome ſalient points of the maſs beneath, and ſeems " a ridge of pendant rock over the vexed abyſs."

This road, the breadth of which differs according to the facility of conſtruction, is in ſome places from twelve to fifteen feet wide, and in others only ten, leaving in general ſpace enough for loaded mules to pass each other; it is paved the greatest part of the way with granite, and is compared, by Mr. Raymond, to a ribband thrown negligently over the mountains.

After winding for some time among these awful scenes, of which no painting can give an adequate description, and of which an imagination the most pregnant in sublime horrors could form but a very imperfect idea, we came within the sound of these cataracts of the Reuss which announced our approach towards another operation of Satanic power, called the Devil's Bridge. We were more struck with the august drapery of this supernatural work, than with the work itself. It seemed less marvellous than expectation had pictured it, and we were perhaps the more disappointed, as we remembered that " the wonderous art pontifical," was a part of architecture with which his infernal majesty was perfectly

fectly well acquainted; and the rocks of the valley of Schellenen were certainly as folid foundations for bridge building as " the aggregated foil folid, or flimy," which was collected amidft the wafte of chaos, and crouded drove " from each fide fhoaling towards the mouth of hell *."

On this fpot we loitered for fome time to contemplate the ftupendous and terrific fcenery. The mountainous rocks lifted their heads abrupt, and appeared to fix the limits of our progrefs at this point, unlefs we could climb the mighty torrent which was ftruggling impetuoufly for paffage under our feet, after precipitating its afflicted waters with tremendous roar in fucceffive cafcades over the disjointed rocks, and filling the atmofphere with its foam.

Separating ourfelves with reluctance

* Paradife Loft, Book x.

from thefe objects of overwhelming greatnefs, we turned an angle of the mountain at the end of the bridge, and proceeded along a way of difficult afcent, which led to a rock that feemed inflexibly to bar our paffage. A bridge faftened to this rock by iron work, and fufpended over the torrent, was formerly the only means of paffing, but numerous accidents led the government to feek another outlet. The rock being too high to climb, and too weighty to remove, the engineer took the middle way, and bored a hole in the folid mafs two hundred feet long, and about ten or twelve feet broad and high, through which he carried the road, The entrance into this fubterraneous paffage is almoft dark, and the little light that penetrates through a crevice in the rock, ferves only to make its obfcurity more vifible. Filled with powerful images of the terrible and fublime, from the enormous objects which I had been contemplating

ing for some hours past, objects, the forms of which were new to my imagination, it was not without a feeling of reluctance that I plunged into this scene of night, whose thick gloom heightened every sensation of terror.

After passing through this cavern, the view which suddenly unfolded itself appeared rather a gay illusion of the fancy than real nature. No magical wand was ever fabled to shift more instantaneously the scene, or call up forms of more striking contrast to those on which we had gazed. On the other side of the cavern we seemed amidst the chaos or the overthrow of nature; on this we beheld her drest in all the loveliness of infancy or renovation, with every charm of soft and tranquil beauty. The rugged and stony interstices between the mountain and the road were here changed into smooth and verdant paths; the abrupt precipice and shagged rock were metamorphosed into gently sloping declivities; the barren and monotonous desert was transformed into a fertile and smiling plain. The long resounding cataract, struggling through the huge masses of granite, here became a calm and limpid current, gliding over fine beds of sand with gentle murmurs, as if reluctant to leave that enchanting abode.

Near the middle of this delicious valley, called the Vale of Urseren, is the village of In-der-Malt, which appeared to have been lately built: behind it was a small forest of pine trees, which are preserved with so much care as a rampart against the avalanches, that the sacred wood was not held more inviolate; and we were told, that the profanation of the axe on this palladium would be followed with the death of the sacrilegious offender.

One

One of my fellow travellers obferved, that this valley, which is three miles in length, and two in breadth, had, according to every appearance, been originally a lake; for which he adduced many mineralogical reafons; and that the drying up of the lake was occafioned by fome violent fraction at the bottom of the valley, which drained the water off from the land, leaving it in its prefent form. Every part of the valley bore marks of high cultivation, if that term can be applied to the culture of meadow lands, where we faw herds of cattle grazing. One production indeed, effentially neceffary for a country fo elevated, was wanting; although the day had been uncommonly beautiful and ferene, and the fun fhed its fofteft rays where we entered this valley, yet the fnows on the higher mountains, and our feelings, when at the clofe of the evening we reached the village of the Hofpital, at the oppofite fide of the valley, reminded us that the moſt acceptable offering our hoſt could make us was, one of thoſe bundles of wood which the villagers are obliged to bring up with great labor and expence from the mountains beneath.

According to popular tradition, this valley was not always ſo unprovided with this article of firſt neceſſity: the mountaineers are perſuaded that their hills were once covered with foreſts, but that ſome magician who dwelt higher up the mountain, or in ſome other place, leſs a paradiſe than their own, not only burnt their woods, but ſo bound the ſoil with potent ſpells, that it has ever ſince been incapable of producing trees. The magician could not have exhibited a more miſchievous ſpecimen of his art to the inhabitants of this valley. Time might indeed have repaired the conflagration, but what exorciſm ſhall reſtore fertility to the enchanted ſoil! Some writers conjecture that

that the wood in this valley was confumed by accident; and that trees grew no more on the fpot, becaufe the winds which fweep irrefiftibly over the heights tear up the young plants before they can take root, being unfheltered by old trees. The greater part of the vallies of Switzerland, it is obferved, wear the fame appearance; the foil occafionally gives way; the trees on the higher ground lofe their footing and flide down; thofe which grow beneath them being no longer fheltered are torn up by winds; and fnow which then accumulates without oppofition on the heights, where thofe forefts ftood, melting at the return of fpring, overwhelms the hills with torrents, dragging away the vegetable earth, and leaving the mountain a fkeleton, unfit for pafturage, or precipitating itfelf in the form of avalanches, deftroys every thing in its courfe,

This valley is under the protection, or rather subject to the Canton of Uri. It formerly made part of the Empire, but the Abbot of Disertis, in the Grisons, possessed various seignorial rights. The house of Austria disposed of its prefecture in the beginning of the fourteenth century, to Henri de L'Hospital, a gentleman of Uri, from whom it was afterwards forcibly transferred, as historians tell us, to Conrad de Moos, another gentleman of the same country. The passage through this valley had often been the subject of contention. At one time the inhabitants, assisted by the Abbot, made war on their neighbours of Uri; at another, aided by their former opponents and two other neighbouring Cantons, they crossed St. Gothard to fight with their present fellow subjects, the inhabitants of the Levantine. Various other disputes having arisen between the inhabitants and the Abbot, which always terminated in bloodshed,

bloodshed, the people who had been indebted to their allies of Uri, for their assistance in the preservation of their liberties, succeeded in the beginning of the fifteenth century in a negociation with the Canton, and relieved themselves for ever of the trouble of taking any farther care of their own privileges, by putting them under the direction of their more powerful neighbours, with a reserve, however, of municipal rights, such as the election of their magistrates, and the trial of civil and criminal causes, subject to the revision of the Canton of Uri.

The valley contains two other villages, besides these already mentioned; and they are the highest social habitations in Europe. The ecclesiastical affairs of the valley are under the direction of the Bishop of Coire, nor has the late revolution interrupted this spiritual intercourse. Formerly the inhabitants

tants chose their priests subject to the confirmation of the bishop, and the Abbot of Disentis, but of late the administrator in holy things is a Capuchin of the Canton.

CHAP. XII.

Top of St. Gothard.—Airolo.

WE paſſed the night at the village of Hoſpital, and the next morning purſued our journey, beginning from hence to aſcend what is properly the mountain of St. Gothard. The ſcene no longer exhibited the ſavage horrors of the chaos we had traverſed the preceding day; the road was neither extremely rapid or dangerous; every where we beheld vegetation, and the mountain myrtle, the white hellebore, and other ſhrubs, indigenous to high regions, were in their bloom. The Reuſs had now ſunk into a rivulet, being no longer fed, as below, by the numerous ſtreams that aſſemble their waters from the hills on each ſide Urſeren; ſometimes it preſented a ſucceſſion of fanciful

ful cafcades, acrofs which one might leap without apprehenfion, even if the foot fhould flip in the enterprife. We had been much affected during the night with cold, and concluded that we had more to fuffer before we gained the fummit; but exercife and the enlivening fun-beams banifhed a fenfation fo new, after having the preceding day felt the heats of July in the valley of Altorf.

We hitherto found that we had indulged a vain expectation of enjoying, from thofe lofty heights, vaft and picturefque views of the countries beneath; fince we had nearly attained what is called the top of St. Gothard, and had yet feen no object that was more remote than the diftance of two leagues. If we looked forward, there appeard nothing but the mountain which we had to climb, and which, having afcended, was fucceeded by another. When we looked back,

back, the mountain we had left was the only object which prefented itfelf, and on either fide our view was confined by thefe wooded precipices, through which, the preceding morning, we had winded our way. Between Urferen and the fummit of St. Gothard, amidft piles of rocks which feemed to forbid all ken beyond, we were, however, gratified with one of thofe burfts through an opening to the north, which difplayed in rich fucceffion the fummits of all the mountains we had paffed, and others at an immenfe diftance, fome gilded by funfhine, and fome enveloped by clouds rolling like a troubled ocean far beneath.

Although the fun poured its noon-tide rays, we perceived that we were afcending into regions of froft, from the appearance, or rather the abfence, of vegetation. The luxuriant pafture of the valley was fucceeded by a coarfe fpiral grafs, which now gave way

way to moſs, or the bare rock, and a ſolitary and ſtunted ſhrub ſometimes protruding itſelf, ſeemed to mark, not ſo much the barrenneſs of the ſoil, as the proſcription of vegetable life.

We at length attained the ſummit of St. Gothard, and were ſaluted on our arrival at the convent by a courteous monk, who came out to welcome us, and invite to take refreſhments. During three or four months in the year theſe Capuchins ſpend their time agreeably enough, and probably there is no ſpot half ſo far out of the reach of the habitable globe, where ſo much variety of amuſement is to be found. Every ſucceſſive gueſt has much to inquire or impart, and here above the world theſe hermits have many opportunities of witneſſing the whimſies and follies with which it abounds. They informed us, that the day before our arrival a numerous retinue of horſes, oxen, mules,

mules, and other cattle, had paſſed in the
ſuite of a great man, whoſe carriage they had
dragged, by his order, from the bottom of
the mountain, that he might have the fame
of croſſing St. Gothard in a vehicle with
wheels. As our countrymen are known to
be the only travelling philoſophers, who
make experiments of this kind, the Monks
had no difficulty in conjecturing on the approach of this long proceſſion, that if it
was not the Emperor, or the burgo-maſter
of Berne, the two greateſt perſonages they had
heard of, it muſt be an Engliſh Lord ; and
they were not miſtaken in their conjecture;
it proved to be an Engliſh Lord, who, for
the reaſons above-mentioned, had run the
riſk of breaking his neck in his mountain
gig, over precipices, which he might have
traverſed without danger on horſeback, or
if he could not ride, in a litter. A tragical
effect of this ſort of temerity had happened
ſome time before to another young Engliſh
nobleman,

nobleman; who, although repeatedly warned by his tutors, that if he attempted to swim down the cataracts of the Rhine, near Rhinfelden, he would inevitably be dashed to pieces, made the fatal experiment, and perished with his companion on the rocks.

In the winter the intercourse of these fathers is confined chiefly to the muleteers, who, at all seasons, traverse these mountains in spite of snows and avalanches. Here the poor traveller, beaten by the tempests, finds repose and nourishment; nor do the Monks demand, even of the wealthy passenger, any recompence for the courtesies they bestow. Every thing that their house affords is set before him with cheerfulness; and he usually returns the hospitality, by leaving on his departure a piece of money under his plate, in order to provide for the relief of travellers, less fortunate than himself. But these pious fathers chiefly maintain this benevolent

nevolent eſtabliſhment, by begging once a year through Switzerland for its ſupport, and well would monaſtic orders have deſerved of mankind, and a ſtronger force than the French revolution would it have required to deſtroy them, had they conſecrated their lives and labors to works of ſimilar uſefulneſs, and thus become the benefactors inſtead of the burdens of ſociety.

The name of Gothard was given to this mountain, according to hiſtorians, before the eſtabliſhment of Chriſtianity, from the Deity worſhipped there, who was ſtiled, as the name imports, the God of the ſummit, or God over all: the canonization of the mountain did not take place till the twelfth century, when Pope Innocent the ſecond made the mountain a ſaint, and, with roman policy, chained the god of the vanquiſhed faith to the car of Chriſtian triumphs.

umphs. Lofty mountains are in scripture called the Mountains of God; and although worship in high-places has been stigmatized as idolatry, yet surely, if the temple, which best delights the Supreme Being, be a temple not made with hands, that which next to the pure and innocent heart is most worthy of his sublimity are the summits of those everlasting mountains, the faint but nearest resemblance on earth of his unchangeablenefs and eternity.

On the top of St. Gothard, one of the most elevated mountains of Europe, we had once imagined the view into Italy on one side, and over Switzerland on the other, would reward all our toil; but this platform, so raised above the level of the earth, is only a deep valley, when compared with the lateral mountains, and skirting-piles of rock that bound the view to this desart, diversified only by the habitation of the
Capuchins,

Capuchins, and the adjoining lakes. Had we even been able to reach any of those rocky summits, which lie on either side, we should have perceived only a chaos of rocks and mountains beneath, with clouds floating at their bases, concealing the rest from our view, and cliffs above covered with untrodden snows; for we were not yet in the region of Glaciers; the eternal ice impended far beyond; and we were told that the mineralogists, or those who go in search of cryftal, which is found in considerable quantities in those mountains, are the only perfons who expofe themselves to the danger of climbing these tremendous precipices. At a little diftance from the Hofpice, we paffed three or four lakes, each about a quarter of a mile long, and of great depth. These lakes are the fources of the Reufs and the Teffino; one of thofe rivers joins the Po, and flows into the Adriatic, the other makes one of the hundred ftreams that fwell the Rhine in its progrefs to the German ocean.

In our rambles near the convent, we faw the remains of a mighty avalanche, which had fo fallen as to form a magnificent bridge over the torrent of the Teffino, the waters having hollowed it below in ftruggling for a paffage; but its furface had yet refifted all the attacks of the fummer fun beams, and feemed as if pleafed with its new habitation, it had there fixed its abode for ever. We walked over this icy bridge to the other fide of the torrent, and fome of my fellow travellers amufed themfelves with a diverfion not very common in the middle of July, that of throwing fnowballs at each other. The temperature of this mountain, the monk told us, was at times various, even in the fame day; but more conftant in general than in the region beneath. Sometimes the Italian zephyr came over them with its genial influence, and conveyed a tranfient fenfation of fummer: fometimes they enjoyed clear fun-fhine on the fummit, when travellers arrived from below drenched in rain; but it appeared from the good man's narrative, that we muft make a winter's fojourn with him to form any adequate idea of the pelting of the pitilefs ftorm during fix or feven months of the year.

We bade adieu to this courteous monk, promifing ourfelves the fatisfaction of fpending a day with him on our return, and began to defcend the mountain on the Italian fide, which, though almoft vertically fteep, is rendered practicable by a well paved road, formed along the fide of the mountain, and which, by its frequent returns, brings the traveller without much inconvenience to the bafe. Although the road was good, the declivity was too great to admit of our trufting ourfelves on horfe-back, efpecially as our horfes had not been accuftomed to travel through fuch mountainous countries. As we loitered down the fteep, the mules we had left behind at the convent overtook us, and we admired the firmnefs with which they trod under their heavy burdens. Mean while a numerous caravan coming from Italy had begun to afcend the fame precipice; and nothing could be more picturefque than the waving picture they prefented, as they moved along the winding path.

I felt fome apprehenfion, that the meeting of fuch a number of mules, with their fides diftended by paniers or wine-cafks, in fo narrow a road, muft be fatal at leaft to one divifion, which I expected to fee tumbling down the precipice from the fhock of the other; but thefe animals, as if confcious of the danger, creep to the utmoft verge of the

the road on either side, and pass each other in long succession without the slightest touch.

After descending a considerable way, we turned to look back on the precipices we had passed. High in air, at a remote distance, we beheld the Tessino on the summit of the mountain, rushing as from the sky over the perpendicular rock. The eye, after losing it for a moment, again catches its daring torrent, rolling over a second precipice, now interrupted in its fall by jutting fragments, now struggling down a declivity of detached masses, broken into various channels. Awhile it vanishes behind the angles of the neighbouring mountains, then forcing its passage through a narrow confine of stupendous granite beneath, dilates and throws itself in one broad foaming sheet over the humbler rocks. Again lost, you see it no more, till it passes silently near the spot whence you gaze, in soft divided

vided streams, that at length, uniting, roll down in a long succession of regular cascades, but little elevated one above the other.

The country around, though barren from its height, wears all the smile of vegetation; the mountains are lofty and romantic, but less terrific as we descend; and so little dangerous are the precipices, that while we were winding along the road, some of our company amused themselves by climbing upon the summits that skirted it, and joined us at a bridge with various specimens of beautiful stones which they had picked up in their rambles. These mountains are rich mines for mineralogists. We had long physical disquisitions about quartz, mica, and schorl, which not being perfectly intelligible to me, I continued to gaze, with untired delight, on the scene around me, while these naturalists marched off to examine
whether

whether an adjoining mountain had moſt ſtrata of white felt-ſpar or green granite. Without much knowledge, however, in the ſcience of ſtones and rocks, the traveller cannot but obſerve with admiration the diverſities of theſe inanimate objects as he paſſes along the road, which, in ſome places, is ſtrewed with theſe variegated minerals, and becomes reſplendent from the ſhivers of ſparkling rock that are waſhed down by the ſtreams from the ſummit of the mountain.

Half way between the convent and the firſt Italian village, is a bridge over the Teſſino, which is ſwelled by a torrent that joins it from a neighbouring precipice, when the river, which for ſome time paſt had flowed tranquilly along, as if ſuddenly impelled by its new companion, re-aſſumes its character of wildneſs, and ruſhes in diſorder

order over the rocks. Here vegetation again ſtruggles into life; the under ſhrubs lift up their meek heads, the tufted roſe of the Alps and the mountain-myrtle waſte their ſweetneſs on the deſart ſcene, and dwarf larch-trees gracefully ſkirt the path. The rapid deſcent to the baſe of the mountain is highly picturefque, the verdant valley beneath, in which Airolo is placed, ſuddenly opened to us ſtrewn with villages, and, when compared with the ſolitudes we had left, preſented a large and beautiful proſpect of human exiſtence; while the gloomy grandeur of the foreſts of dark pines on one ſide, and the view acroſs the valley of leſſer mountains, whoſe laſt ſnows were diſſolving in the ſummer ray on the other, form altogether a ſcene where ſublimity and grace blend in ſolemn harmony.

We entered into the Levantine valley at Airolo,

Airolo, which is a confiderable village, or rather a fmall town at the foot of St. Gothard, handfomely built of ftone, and the chief entrepot or warehoufe for all goods that pafs between this part of Switzerland and Italy.

The adventurous fpirit of commerce, fearlefs of the hanging precipice, the falling avalanche, and the yawning gulph, firft traced the daring path acrofs this mountain, the higheft, after Mont Blanc, in Europe, and has thus connected, by the foft ties of civilization, two countries, between which nature feemed to have placed an infurmountable barrier. A fmart girl, the daughter of the innkeeper at Airolo, fpoke of herfelf as one of the mountain favages, with an air fo gracefully coquettifh, and in fuch pure Italian; as convinced us that fhe would have been much mortified had we affected to credit her affertion. She reminded

minded me of an expreffion I had read in one of Rouffeau's unpublifhed letters to the former Marchionefs de C——, " that he had quitted Paris to go and civilize himfelf in the woods."

CHAP. XIII.

Valley of Levantine.—Torrents of the Teſſino.—Harveſt-home.

AFTER leaving Airolo, we journeyed for ſome hours on a fine level road, which, from our late perpendicular travelling, we found a very agreeable relief. The Teſſino partakes alſo of the gentleneſs of the plain, and being joined on its entrance into the valley by the torrents that flow from the Glaciers on the eaſtern ſide, which ſeparate this country from the Haut Vallais, rolls along an ample river, and is ſtill fed in its progreſs by tributary ſtreams from the lofty mountains that divide the Levantine from the Griſons on one ſide, and the valleys of Locarno and Maggia on the other. The ruſhing of waters on our right as we paſſed along,

along, led us to penetrate through a little grove of alder-trees to the river, where we beheld one of thefe torrents paying its homage to the Teffino in a manner fingularly graceful. Swelled by the heat on the upper mountains beyond its ufual volume, it rolled impetuoufly down its narrow channel, and difdaining its accuftomed barrier of a rock, by which divided into two ftreams it flowed on each fide into the river; now rufhing with a fuller tide of waters, it bounded over the obftacle which it could not difplace, and mingled itfelf with the Teffino at an ample diftance, after defcribing a lofty and beautifully feathered arch. The upper part of this valley is chiefly devoted to pafturage, but we found the peafants in fome places drying their corn, which operation is performed by fufpending the fheafs on long poles arranged horizontally above each other, and tyed to others that are ftuck in the ground. There

was

was a lightnefs and grace in the ruftic movements of thefe fubject Italians, which their mafters on the other fide of St. Gothard had not yet acquired. At the diftance of every quarter of a mile in the nooks of mountains, and on the edge of precipices, the white fpire lifts its ftately head, and gives you, amidft fcenes of favage wildnefs, a glimpfe of civilization. Secluded amidft thofe alpine heights from the reft of mankind, religion feems to be the fole intellectual pleafure of the inhabitants of thefe defarts, and the flow founds of the frequent bell that, amidft the clefts of the rocks knolls to church, is heard with a foothing fenfation by the mufing traveller, flinging its foft vibrations on the mountain echoes.

The clofing evening brought us to the houfe where a toll is received for paffage, and which we found alfo a very pleafant and comfortable inn.

Having

Having accompanied the Teſſino ſince our departure from Airolo, flowing ſometimes on our right, and ſometimes on our left, with a gentle and ſteady courſe; we ſuppoſed that the youthful ſpirit with which it had bounded over its native regions being now ſobered, it would continue to purſue, with an even current, " the noiſeleſs tenor of its way." The loud roar of many waters, as we alighted from our horſes at Dazio, led us to catch the laſt lingering ſhades of twilight, and follow thoſe powerful ſounds. Having advanced a few paces, we perceived that the ſpacious valley through which we had travelled, was abruptly cloſed by ſtupendous perpendicular rocks, that left no other opening than a narrow channel with a ſpace gained from it by human induſtry to form a road between its maſſy walls and the torrent. The waters which had begun to ſtruggle for paſſage above a bridge which is thrown acroſs the ſtream, were

were now tortured into a thousand forms. Here a mass of rock of enormous size in the midst of the channel raised the river at once from its bed, pouring it impetuously into a deep bason with tremendous roar; there a rifted cleft, the only outlet to the waters, increased their fury, and dashing against the rocks with redoubled force, broke the torrent into different currents, and filled the atmosphere with particles of its foam. The enormous masses of rock sometimes lifted erect their bold and savage shapes, and sometimes, where they had been hollowed out to form the road, towered at an immense height over the path and the torrent with such threatening aspect, that I could not pass beneath without feeling an involuntary shudder, which was heightened by the approaching darkness. Below the frowning brow of the rocks, hanging groves of pine and fir bend majestically from the cliffs, while the graceful larch-tree decorates the banks,

banks, and the weeping birch bends far over the ſtream and mingles its long branches with the agitated waters. The rapidity of the deſcent is communicated to the river, and a ſucceſſion of ſweeping caſcades, that ruſh in every imaginary form down a channel, worn at a fearful depth below the level of the road, leads to a bridge which ſeemed hung in air over the gulph, but of which we could only catch an imperfect glimpſe, ſince the laſt ſhades of evening had now fallen on the ſcene, and we trod back our ſteps up the winding brink of the torrent, not without the deepeſt impreſſions of awe ſoftened by admiration.

On our return we found Dazio the reſidence of mirth and gaiety. It was the harveſt-home of the maſter of the inn, and, as we paſſed to our apartments, a chorus met our ear that ſeemed to burſt from ſome throats more tuneful than thoſe of peaſants.
With

With the licence allowed to travellers, we joined the feſtive throng, and were not a little amuſed with the manner in which this harmonious circle was compoſed. The chief of the band, and moſt illuſtrious of the gueſts, were half a dozen merry Italian prieſts, who, it was evident, from their rubicund faces and ſparkling looks, had been conſulting other poets than thoſe whoſe hymns were to be found in their breviaries or maſs-books. Great allowances muſt be made for national cuſtoms, but the appearance of ſo many holy men thrilling out amorous love-ſongs, and chanting bacchanalian glees, although with voices harmoniouſly tuned, and confiderable force of execution, did not a little ſurpriſe us, who were accuſtomed to the gravity and reſerve of the clerical character in other countries. We were, however, led to ſuppoſe that theſe prieſts had not overſtepped the bounds here allowed to their profeſſion, from the delighted and respectful attention with which the rustics around listened to their melody; nor is it probable they would have indulged themselves in this gay demeanor, at the risk of exciting a sentiment of irreverence towards their persons.

In the morning we went to take another view of this region of nature's marvels; day-light had diminished something of its terror, and we surveyed its savage graces with renewed astonishment and rapture; the rocky fragments now glittered in the sun, and the deep blue Italian sky spread its lovely canopy over this scene of lavish beauty. After passing the aërial bridge, of which we had caught a distant glimpse the preceding evening, we journeyed down a steep but well-constructed road on the edge of the Tesino, which rolled along its narrow bed, if not with all the daring boldness of its mountain course, at least with sufficient

sufficient turbulence to seize the delighted attention, while the unwearied eye alternately wandered from the rapid waters to the picturesque drapery of their banks.

As we proceeded, the valley extended itself in breadth, and admitted of various kinds of cultivation, amongst which we remarked that of the purple vines, beneath whose broad leaves and pendant clusters, dropping from festoons arched over our heads as we passed along the road, we found relief from the parching heat of the midday sun, while we looked up to the snowy mountains which bounded this scene of summer, with a feeling of something like regret that we were out of the reach of their frigid influence.

CHAP. XIV.

Government of the Levantine Valley.

THE Levantine Valley contains several well-built villages, and the number of inhabitants, who are all Italians, is computed at about twelve thousand. They have in general a look of intelligence, and something of mountain-independence in their manner; but are under complete subjection to the democracy of the Canton of Uri. The valley is divided into eight vicinanze or districts, about a league each in extent. The village of Faido, which is situated in the midst of the Valley, is the residence of the bailiff or governor, who is elected to this office by the Canton of Uri, or who, rather agreeably to the established mode of election in these democracies, purchases the place of his fellow citizens, who know too well the value

value of money not to make a good bargain of their rights. Once in four years the inhabitants of this Valley behold the cortege of their new sovereign descending from St. Gothard, perhaps with somewhat of the same sensations as the defenceless timid bird views the downward flight of the pouncing hawk, darting on his prey.

These rustic monarchs of Uri, in coming to govern a people, of whose language, manners and customs they are ignorant, do not appear to be animated by the ambition, which led Cæsar to wish rather to be the first man in a village than the second at Rome. They have more solid views than those of power; that of replenishing their treasury, exhausted in rewards to their brother sovereigns for their free suffrages; and no sooner are they installed at *Barataria,* than fines, exactions, and rapacities of every kind follow in their train, and every resistance to lawful authority meets with condign punishment: as the history of each of these subject vallies can tell, the hearts of whose inhabitants have sometimes swelled beyond endurance at the extortion of their harpy governors.

The people of the Valley revolted against their sovereign of Uri in the beginning of this century, and obtained certain privileges, which their descendants, by another revolt, thirty or forty years since, have imprudently forfeited. Stung into disobedience by some act of proconsular tyranny, they took up arms against their sovereign, and put themselves into a most open and daring insurrection. The Canton of Schweitz had, on a former occasion, undertaken to reduce the insurgents, and had succeeded; but the present rebellion bore symptoms so alarming, that the whole of the Cantons armed to bring the Valley to obedience. Agreeably to to the maxims of moſt governments, that the governors are always in the right, and the governed in the wrong, no Canton can interfere in any diſputes between the ſovereign and the ſubjects, unleſs to puniſh the preſumption of the latter.

The whole Helvetic body felt the cauſe of the ſovereign of Uri to be their own, and with heart and hand, with an alacrity worthy of the cauſe, coaleſced together to put a deciſive ſtop to ſuch heretical and dangerous pretenſions. Had the rebels only had to contend with their maſters of Uri, it is poſſible they might have ſhaken their authority; but when the inſurgents beheld the cohorts of every regular government in Switzerland pouring down from the mountains in warlike array; heard the loud blaſt of their trumpets, repeated by a thouſand echoes amidſt their cliffs and rocks; ſaw terror in the van, and annihilation in the rear; they

they very prudently gave up a conteft, which muft have ended in their utter deftruction.

The grievances of the infurgents were redreffed in the mode that might rationally be expected: their form of government, and all their laws were abolifhed, and they were deprived of every privilege, municipal, civil, and judicial: the ufe of arms, to which every Swifs is accuftomed, however low his rank in the fcale of fociety, was ftrictly forbidden, and this fage precaution has perpetuated their dominion, by deftroying, not only the means, but the knowledge of refiftance, fince he who never handles arms muft remain ignorant of the exercife.

Thus the former fubjects of the Levantine Valley became the unrefifting flaves of their citizen-fovereigns, and the bailiff of Uri is now their fole adminiftrator, lawgiver,

giver, and judge. No one indeed can dispute the right of this Canton, and its allies, to reduce thefe rebels to obedience, fince the charter of their fervitude is clearly eftablifhed by every document of hiftory. In ancient times they were probably, like other mountaineers, wild, and free: but in the twelfth century the country belonged to bifhops, then to the chapter of Milan; and in the fourteenth century Charles the Fourth mortgaged his imperial prefecture for a trfling fum to Conrad or John Moos; the fame perfonage, who had before monopolized the prefecture of Urferen. The canons of Milan, to rid themfelves of the fatigues of government, gave up their ecclefiaftical titles to their duke by whom they were tranfmitted in the middle of the fifteenth century, on what conditions we know not, to the Canton of Uri, who have ever fince prudently kept poffeffion. It therefore clearly appears, that whether governed

verned by bishops, emperors, chapters, canons, John Moos, dukes or democrats, the inhabitants of the Levantine have always, since the twelfth century, been either subjects or serfs.

While the Canton of Uri takes care of the civil concerns of the inhabitants of this Valley, the archbishop of Milan administers to their spiritual necessities : being judge in all ecclesiastical disputes, with the privilege of placing his vicar general as rector in the seminary at Faido. Now, as the Archbishop of Milan, under every political change, preserves the sanctity of his character, he must no doubt continue archbishop, whether it be as Pontiff under the Emperor of Germany, or as simple citizen of the Cisalpine Republic. Whatever degree of fraternity, therefore, may in future exist between this Republic, and that of Uri, it is to be presumed, that no slight care will be taken by the

the latter to prevent the admiffion of thofe principles, which have found their way into Lombardy, fince if ever thefe principles fhould overleap their prefent geographical boundary, and become points of confcience with the fubjects of the Valley, the Canton of Uri will perhaps in vain apply to this republican archbifhop to anathematize their difobedience.

CHAP

CHAP. XV.

Government of the Canton of Uri.—Origin of Swiss Freedom.

HAVING traced this short sketch of the manner in which the democratic Cantons of Switzerland govern their subjects, it will perhaps be proper to relate, in a few words, the manner in which they govern themselves.

The government of the Cantons of Uri, Schweitz, and Underwalden, is said to be democratic. These states were once, like other parts of Switzerland, dependent on the empire, and whether they were deemed from their situation not worth the labour of conquest, or were comprehended in that policy which engaged the princes of the empire

empire to grant special immunities to various cities and districts, the inhabitants of these wild countries enjoyed the privilege of chusing their own magistrates, and being governed by their own laws. This liberty, however, was sometimes restrained by the presence of an emperor's bailiff, who resided amongst them as supreme judge in criminal cases, and possessed other imperial prerogatives. From some neglect of those governors, it happened that the Cantons were often left to their own administration, and in one of these intervals we find, from history, they united together in the beginning of the twelfth century, in defence of their rights, against the unjust attacks of the monks of the famous Abbey of Einsidlen. In vain did civil power come in aid of ecclesiastical thunders. Neither the ban of the empire, nor the excommunication of the church, could shake, even in those ages of darkness and servitude, the intrepid minds

of

of these mountaineers; and their resistance to the monks, the emperor, and the church, was, after a struggle of thirty or forty years, crowned with success. Their leagues, offensive or defensive, with each other, could not, however, preserve their independence. In spite of their petitions and remonstrances, Rodolphe, Count of Hapsbourg, was sent in the beginning of the thirteenth century, by the Emperor, Otho the Fourth, as imperial prefect; and it appears, from the good understanding between these Cantons, and the successor of the Emperor, Frederick the Second, that their chains were not worn with an ill grace, nor was their assistance to him in his Italian wars less chearfully given from his being then under the sentence of papal excommunication.

The death of this emperor, in the middle of the thirteenth century, having thrown the empire into long confusion, the inhabitants of these Cantons, instead of taking advantage of the troubles, and regaining their late short-lived independence, chose for their captain-general, defender, or governor, another Rodolphe, Count of Hapsbourg. It appears, however, that the Count performed essential services to these Cantons, and when he was named to the purple, confirmed or bestowed on them various privileges; but during the reign of his ambitious son they obtained their independence. Albert had succeeded in bringing several adjoining Cantons under his dominion; the town of Zurich alone resisted his solicitations and menaces, and was defended, in 1299, with valour and effect by the Abbess, who was governess of the town, and who disdained to submit to the House of Austria. Various were the expedients made use of by the new Emperor to engage the inhabitants of the three Cantons to surrender their privileges, and purchase their tranquillity by obedience; and many were the outrages to which they had submitted from proconsular tyrants under the name of bailiffs, who were sent amongst them with as little ceremony, and with equal right, as their own officers of the same description are now deputed to regulate the concerns of their Levantine subjects. At length the three heroes, Stauffach, Furst, and Arnold, formed their renowned conspiracy against the tyrant, and on the first day of the year 1307, liberated their country, by seizing and sending out of their territory all their imperial governors. Their liberty was not obtained without a struggle; the battle of Morgarten, in which the Austrians were routed by an inconsiderable number of Swifs, brought on the confederation at Brunnen, and laid the foundation for the adhesion of the other Cantons, which successively joined the alliance, and the spirit of freedom proved a more powerful barrier

against

against the House of Austria, than even their rocks or their mountains.

Each Canton, on the acquisition of its independence, chose its own form of government, and the three Cantons who first freed themselves from the yoke, made choice of that in which the supreme power resides essentially in the people. Each individual who has attained the age of fourteen years, forms a member of the sovereignty, who meet every year on the first of May in a general council of the nation, in order to form laws and elect magistrates. The executive power is entrusted to a regency, who, under this annual salutary inspection, are no doubt careful to administer their government in such a manner, as to meet their representatives the ensuing year without the dread of censure.

The inhabitants of this Canton are esteemed, by early historians, for the politeness

liteness and sincerity of their manners towards strangers; but the accounts given by later writers are very contradictory to this observation. Madame de Sillery, who, after her banishment from France, resided some months in one of these democratic Cantons, asserts, that there is no other country in the world where strangers are so ill-treated. It is probable, however, that travellers in general would meet with more kindness than fell to the lot of Madame Sillery, who had acted too distinguished a part in the French Revolution to have any claims to a cordial reception in these Cantons. We were ourselves warned to conceal carefully on our journey that we had any relation with France.

The truth is, that the inhabitants of the democratic Cantons of Switzerland are under the dominion of a power far more absolute than that exercised by the privileged classes

classes of the great Cantons. This power is superstition, and with the aid of this mighty engine, which molds the passions at will, the priests have atchieved still more than the aristocracy, and have represented the French as apostates, that war not merely with earth, but with heaven. No other part of Switzerland is so unenlightened, and consequently so hostile to the spirit of true liberty, as these little Cantons, where democracy and despotism march under the same banners; for although the government is democratic, the number of those who have a right to a seat in the general assembly is inconsiderable, compared with the numbers that are excluded.

It is computed by a late writer, that the population of the three Cantons of Uri, Schweitz, and Underwalden, with the democracies of Zug and Glaris, amount to no more than eighty-three thousand souls, and furnish only twenty thousand active citizens; while the countries over which they hold sole or divided authority, contain a population of three hundred and thirty-seven thousand. The government, therefore, though democratic with respect to those individuals who make a part of the sovereignty, is to the unprivileged inhabitants of the Cantons, and to its subjects in the bailiwicks, a confirmed hereditary aristocracy; and while in other countries the different classes of society are separated from each other by different habitudes, which makes the evil of subordination less felt here, where the reigning and the subject class are the equal companions of each others childhood, the latter must perceive with peculiar bitterness, as they approach to manhood, that they are destined to no share of the boasted liberty of their country; but that if born on the northern side of the mountain of St. Gothard, they are subjects,

jects, and if on the southern they are
slaves.

Avarice, as well as superstition, has
contributed to render the people of the little
Cantons hostile to the French Revolution,
an event which has interrupted the interchange of those friendly courtesies which,
before that period, passed between France
and those Cantons. We cannot be much
surprised that the aristocratical Cantons of
Switzerland felt little sympathy in the establishment of French equality; but we might
perhaps have expected more congenial sentiments in governments, the existence of
which conveys a tacit approbation at least of
the sovereignty of the people, till we are
informed that France, while a monarchy,
paid a tribute to these sovereigns, which
the great Cantons had indignantly rejected.
Each male child of the three democratic
Cantons received from the day of its birth

six livres annually, and the magistrates were paid in proportion. The exchange was fair, money for friendship. The French republicans have broken the treaty, no more money is paid, and no more friendship is returned; and these democrats are as much incensed at this violation of the compact, as if their own subjects had broken their allegiance.

It requires no great penetration to discover that the abuses which exist in these Swiss governments will be corrected, not so much perhaps from the struggles of the oppressed, as from the conviction in those who govern, how much it behoves their interest to loosen the reins of arbitrary power. The history of every country is full of examples how fatal to tyranny is the burst of the heart that swells against oppression. But without recurring to classic story, the Swiss have only to consult their own annals, when

by

by the valorous feats of their immortal ancestors,

> "Forth from his eyric rouzed in dread
> "The ravening eagle northward fled;"
>
> COLLINS.

and they will probably reflect that the age of heroism is not past with that of chivalry; but that those who march in the steps of an Albert, may find in their path a Verner de Stauffaken, or a William Tell.

CHAP. XVI.

Giornico.— Bellinezone.— Mount Cenave.— Lugano.— Lake of Lugano.

After leaving the town of Faido, we continued our route along the valley, ever prefenting fome fcene of wild, folemn, majeftic beauty, over which the eye wandered with unwearied delight; of which the picture is indelibly graven on the imagination, and which memory recals with foothing rapture; but when the pen would trace thofe images which glow upon the heart, it is found unfaithful to the purpofe! How impoffible to convey an adequate idea of thofe varied, thofe coloffal regions, compared to which all other fcenery is tame and diminutive, all other objects are "flat, ftale, and unprofitable."

STATE OF SWITZERLAND. 219

The beautiful little town of Giornico, which we paffed, is famous for a victory gained by the Swifs, the latter end of the fifteenth century, over one of the Sforzas, duke of Milan, who, difcontented with the ceffion made of this valley by his anceftors, came to reconquer the territory. Some of the artillery taken in this engagement are here preferved as trophies. When we came to Pollezio, we were once more on even ground. This is the laft diftrict of the valley, and compared with the upper part, is of confiderable breadth, bearing all the productions of flat countries. The Teffino increafed by numerous ftreams, fwelled by the torrent flowing from Monte Ucello, and no longer confined between beds of rocks that refift its impetuofity, frequently inundates the lower part of this valley, called Riviera, the Valley of the River, and which is marfhy, and unwholefome.

Further on, the waters of the Moefa, rufhing in a cataract from the mountains of the Grifons, pour themfelves into the Teffino, which now rolls on with gentle courfe, a broad and ample river till it forms the Lago Magiore. We croffed the river of the Grifons, and entered on the territory of Bellinzone, and after paffing through two or three pleafant villages, hid amidft the purple feftoons, hanging from the trees ripe for the vintage, and which had a more picturefque appearance than the huge ftatues of St. Chriftopher, with which they were decorated by the piety of the inhabitants, we came within fight of the town.

Bellinzone is fituated near the foot of Mount Cenere, and is alfo bounded by that chain of foftened hills, which ranged in wild diforder, feparate the lower valley of the Levantine from the Swifs bailiwicks of Maggia and Locarno. Three caftles, erected ed on lofty heights, frown over the walls of the city, and are fucceffively the refidence of the bailiffs of the three democratic Cantons of Uri, Schweitz, and Underwalden, to which Bellinzone and its dependencies are fubject. We had now entirely quitted every thing that was Swifs, except their dominion, and found a confiderable change, not only in the manners, but in the phyfiognomy of the people. The women have here the fine expreffion of the Madona countenance; fomething of which had firft ftruck us at Lucerne; and in the men, we obferved the robuft form of the mountaineer foftened by a look of Italian civilization. We were alfo reminded of our approach to Italy, by a coarfe imitation of its tafte in the plaiftered piazza, the gilt balcony, and the painted Corinthian pillars, with which the houfes were decorated. The principal church, a building of fine conftruction, rich in ornaments, and a confiderable

able number of religious edifices, give an air of dignity to the place. After repoſing ourſelves a ſhort time at Bellinzone, we haſtened to Lugano, being deſirous to ſee the ceremony of the inſtallation of the governor, which was to take place within a few days.

Our road to this town lay acroſs Mount Cenere, the laſt of that chain of mountains, formerly called the Rhetian Alps, which divide the Griſons from the Valtaline, and other parts of Italy. Having travelled about a league along the valley on the ſouth of Bellinzone, we began to climb the ſteep aſcent of Mount Cenere; and as we journeyed in the mid-day ſun, ſhould have been much incommoded by the heat, had not the luxuriant branches of the cheſnut, which grows to a prodigious ſize, and in the moſt laviſh profuſion on this mountain, ſpread a friendly ſhelter over our path.

The

The woods of Mount Cenere, we were told, were the haunts of robbers, who find a refuge from juftice in their wild receffes, and alfo from this mountain being a frontier, of which the legal jurifdiction is uncertain. Its fouthern promontory ftretching to the river, which joins the lakes of Lugano and Locarno, is fo infefted by ferpents, that at this feafon of the year, neither men or cattle could approach it without danger. Half way up this mountain foreft, we were prefented with a noble view over the Lago Maggiore, the great lake, to Locarno, and faw in the back-ground the lofty mountains rifing to Glaciers, which feparate the Vallais from Italy. After a ride of three hours, having gained the fummit, we began to defcend into a lovely paftoral country, which opened to our view on the oppofite fide. The Alps were here foftened into hills, which, when not covered with hanging woods, wore the appearance of

of the moſt ſmiling cultivation, and diſ-
played in beautiful ſucceſſion, thoſe varying groupes of picturesque objects with
which the landſcape painter delights to decorate his ſcene. Along this valley, called
the Valley of Agano, runs a ſmall rivulet,
bearing away the laſt ſnows from the Ga-
moghera, which lifts high in the diſtance
its pyramidal head, and is the central point
of the frontier mountains, ſtretching in various directions from the Valteline, the Griſons, and the Italian bailiwicks: its ſummit, we were told, commands a magnificent view, not only over thoſe mountainous regions, but which, piercing beyond
them, extends as far as the city of Milan,
the cathedral of which may be ſeen from
that elevated point.

After a delicious ride through this romantic and peopled valley, we came in view of
the lake and town of Lugano, where we
ſoon

soon arrived, and were informed, that the
auguft ceremony of the inftallation of the
governor was to take place on the following day. In the mean time we found, that
the magnificent and fovereign lords of the
the Cantons, who vifit on thefe occafions the
chief feat of ultra-montaine jurifdiction,
had taken poffeffion of all the great apartments of the principal inn, where we had
alighted, and where they were deliberating
in full affembly on various weighty matters
of government, and unravelling knotty
points of civil and contentions concern, to
the determination of which the ordinary
knowledge of the municipal authorities of
their jurisdiction was confidered as incom-
petent or unfatisfactory. As this was not a
part of the ceremony which appeared the
moft interefting, we hired a felucca in order to pafs the remainder of the afternoon
on the lake, and view its enchanting fcenery. The lake, which is extremely irregular,

forms on that part, where the town is situated, a fine bay, along which, to a confiderable extent, elegant villas and airy pavillions are profufely fcattered, fupported by light arcades, and long fweeps of Corinthian pillars, combining all the graceful proportions of Grecian architecture, with the enchanting drapery of the landfcape. In the clumfy country-feats, belonging to no order whatever, on the other fide of the Alps, we had feen art at war with nature, and deforming with the heavy manfion, and the ftiff parterre, fcenes, where every natural object bore the print of uncultivated beauty; and the only picturefque edifices we had beheld excited a gloomy emotion: fuch were the thick-walled Gothic caftles, perched high on the tremendous cliffs, frowning with fullen afpect over the fubject plain, and recalling the chearlefs images of feudal times. While the polifhed ftructures that decorate the lovely bay of Lugano

Lugano prefent the fair images of Attic tafte, together with the idea of that country, for ever dear to the lovers of the elegant arts, where, after the long night of barbarifm, they once more revived to embellifh with perennial flowers the path of life, and exalt our nature, while they blefs our exiftence.

Thofe beautiful retreats, which adorn the bay, belong chiefly to wealthy and noble families of Milan *; many of whom, either preferved their original inheritance, or purchafed lands in this bailiwick: and by

* One of the manfions, in the neighbourhood of Lugano, is inhabited by Madame Beccaria, the daughter of the illuftrious Beccaria, who inherits from her father an underftanding of the firft clafs, and unites with the graces of perfon, and the moft charming fimplicity of manners, that independence of foul, and love of rational liberty, which is the characteriftic of fuperior minds.

acquiring the right of citizenship in these privileged, though dependent districts, found a refuge from the civil diforders of their own country. Some of these summer mansions seem to impend over the lake, while others fall back gracefully behind luxuriant gardens, that descend in gentle slopes to the level of the waters. Those cultivated spots, perfuming the air with the fragrant blossoms of orange and lemon trees, together with the view of the first chain of hills above Lugano, covered with the vine, the almond, the fig, and the olive, convey to the English traveller the agreeable idea of a richer climate, and a more favoured sky. The frequent steeples lift their pointed heads amidst forests and hanging woods of variegated trees, and far in the back-ground huge and lofty mountains rising into Alps, part of which were capt with snows, seemed to frown with savage but impotent severity

rity on the glowing and fertile landscape, that circled the limpid lake beneath.

On the left of Lugano, the lake runs a considerable length beyond the Swifs territory into the dominions of the Emperor, and the Valteline, of which we beheld the villages skirting the waters below projecting rocks.

Having landed on the shore opposite Lugano, where the mountains rise abrupt from the lake, shagged with rock and wood, we entered some of these oval retreats, which the inhabitants have formed under the shelter of excavated cliffs, for the preservation of their wines from the summer heats: some of the owners of those wines were on the spot, and cordially invited us to taste their delicious flavor and coolness. The sun setting over these hills, and burnishing the lake with its long reflected beams,

beams, warned us to return. We defcended from the ridge of the mountain, where we had gone to view the flow of a playful torrent, and joined a mufical fleet of Milanefe ladies and gentlemen, who were failing to Lugano to be prefent at the inftallation.

CHAP.

CHAP. XVII.

Inſtallation of the Bailiff of Lugano.—Italian Odes.—Sail down the Lake.—Locarno.

THE following day was uſhered in by a concert of bells from every ſteeple in the town and neighbourhood. The ſtreets were crouded with well-dreſſed people of both ſexes, who had come from various parts of the country, and beyond the lake, to celebrate the gay feſtival. After breakfaſt the magnificent deputies of the laudable Helvetic Body marſhalled themſelves in order, and preceded by their heralds, ſtandard-bearers, trumpeters, and other attendants, marched in proceſſion up the hill to the great church of St. Lugano, where this ſolemn ceremony was to take place. There we found a numerous aſſemblage of ladies

ladies and gentlemen dreſſed with elegance, ſome of whom had taken poſſeſſion of the pulpit, reading-deſk, and altar, and were liſtening with polite attention to the uncouth ſounds which iſſued from the aiſle below, and which muſt have ſeemed barbarous diſſonance to the delicacy of an Italian ear. Thoſe inharmonious accents proceeded from the lips of the Recorder of the bailiwick, or the clerk of the magnificent deputation, who was reading, in the Swiſs language, to the new ſovereign, the laws, cuſtoms, and regulations, by which he was to govern, during two years, the noble town and diſtrict of Lugano. For the benefit of thoſe who were to be governed, and that no poſſibility of colluſion might take place, the ſame engagement which the new governor had taken in German, he took afterwards in Italian. No ſooner had this double act been properly adminiſtered, and the people once more ſecure in the poſſeſſion

of

their governor, than the vaults of the church refounded with the cries of *Viva! Viva!* long live our gracious bailiff, and the moft illuftrious deputies of the magnificent Cantons of Switzerland; to which affectionate exclamation, in the filver founds of Italian, German refponfes were poured forth by the deputation, of long live the noble city and bailiwick of Lugano!

That the deputation, with cordial fincerity, fhould pray for long life and health to the noble town of Lugano, was perfectly natural; the motives to a reciprocal attachment, on the part of the bailiwick, are fomewhat lefs evident.

In the beginning of the fixteenth century, Maximilian Sforza, Duke of Milan, made a donation of the territory of Lugano to the Swifs, for the aid they gave him in driving the French out of Italy, and which was

was confirmed three years after by Francis the Firſt, when he made peace with the Cantons, whom he had defeated at the famous battle of Marignan. As the Swifs received the gift unincumbered with any conditions, ſuch as privileges, rights, or immunities, in favour of the people, ſo they have religiouſly handed it down unchanged to their poſterity. The power of the bailiff is almoſt unlimited. He is the repreſentative and co-ſovereign with the Cantons, the fountain of all honor, power, and glory, ſole judge in all civil and criminal matters, but aſſiſted in his important functions by a ſyndical, a ſecretarial, a lieutenant bailiff, and other officers, ſo that no complaint ſhould exiſt among the people of a ſcarcity of perſons to govern them.

The municipal regulations, however, of the towns and villages in the bailiwicks, are entruſted to perſons choſen by the inhabitants,

bitants, but no laws are enacted that are not in perfect accord with the will of the sovereign, and submitted to his sanction.

The stated revenue of these bailiwicks is unfortunately not very considerable, and the emoluments of the bailiffs chiefly arise from speculations on the display of the worst passions of our nature, such as fines in criminal cases. Much cannot be said of the paternal protection given to that state, where the governors become rich in proportion as their subjects become wicked. Such sort of financial speculations, we were told, are too frequently to be found in the history of Swifs proconsular administration; the latitude of power being almost unbounded, and the love of money being proverbially the sin which most easily besets those sovereigns, it is not surprizing that the merit of disinterestedness should be uncommon.

" The

"The avidity of their governors," we are informed by one of their apologists, "when it passes its *just* bounds, has been very often repressed by the sydictorial deputies, who are sent to regulate the accounts." What are the *just* bounds of a Swiss bailiff's avidity is not precisely marked, but there is reason to believe that it is not punished by these fraternal deputies with extreme severity.

The same author laments that the inhabitants of these bailiwicks are much addicted to chicane, and that frequent law-suits disturb the peace of families. This taste for legal contention is the more singular, as the disputants are deprived of one considerable pleasure in the controversy, which is, the knowledge of the language in which they contend, all civil causes being tried in German. The bailiffs, who in general are ignorant of the Italian, are always attended

by

by interpreters; but who shall translate, for the benefit of the Italian client, the wordy war of German attornies?

Whatever grounds of complaint from proconsular rapacity might have existed in former times, we were happy to hear, amidst universal plaudits, of the return of the golden age under the administration of the most illustrious Signor Don Francesco Saverio Zeltner, counsellor and captain of artillery of the most excellent city and republic of Soleure, who now terminates his most upright government of captain regent of Lugano. The administration of this renewed governor was celebrated in odes, sonnets, and other poetical records, which were distributed in the church with great profusion at the close of the ceremonial. No Horace or Waller could string the lyre with fonder raptures to the glories of Augustus or Cromwell, than that which burst from the poets of Lugano in praise of their immortal bailiff. The names of heroes who lived before Agamemnon have perished, we are told, in unknown night, because unsung by the sacred bard; but the name of Don Zeltner is proudly rescued from such vulgar oblivion. We shall pass over the eulogium of the tribe of poets by profession, to whom fiction is allowed as a matter of right, and shall only slightly mention the strains of the "Signor Abate Don Amatore Solari, proregent, professor extraordinary," and enjoying numerous other titles, who had put a new string to his old discordant harp,

"Da nuovo plettro l'agitata corda,
"Tutte di Zeltner le virtù ricorda,

to record the train of Zeltner's virtues; we shall not consider too deeply the sorrows of the noble fiscal Signor Don Pietro Frasca; doctor

doctor of both laws, who demands of his mournful muse, and not inelegantly—why, with dishevelled hair, she beats her snowy bosom, and who answers, by her sighs, striking on her lyre; " sospiri all' etra— Ma aimé ch 'ei parte"—That Zeltner, the great hero, is about to depart. Nor shall we dwell long on the everlasting ode of the thrice gallant Capuchin P. C. A. Griconi, who, while others are tuning the string to the praises of the illustrious Zeltner, is warbling, with no less harmony, the peerless accomplishments of the most lovely Signora Donna Orsola Zeltner, his wife: not forgetting, in the hurry of his pindarics, that the God of War had entrusted to the husband

" A te fulmini et falangi
" Marte affida,"

his thunder and phalanxes; for which Signor Prelsoechi accounts in his Anacreontics,

tics, by assuring us, that Don Zeltner is not of mortal mold;

> "Dal ciel costui discende
> "No che mortal non é;"

but that he came to Lugano, "Dal Regno degli Dei," from the empyrium of the Gods.

Poor is even praise like this, when compared with the poetical tribute, which the virtues of Zeltner have wrung from the brain of the venerable college of respectable and worshipful notaries of Lugano, the bankers, trustees, and attornies of every individual in the state; who overleaping the dull, precise, plodding forms of law "be it known to all men," and "by these presents," strike the soft chords of poetic eulogy, and in lays appropriate to their professions, so far as their professions can sympathize with lays, pour forth a panegyric on on the rare difinterestedness and exalted worth of Capt. Zeltner.

" When Alexander," fing these tuneful notaries, " when Alexander returned from the vanquished Euphrates, loaded with gold to his native country, and followed by his armed hosts, sighs of sorrow broke forth from the bottom of his heart; the bones of Achilles, which he contemplated on his way, awoke the ungrateful recollection of the Achean trumpet, and excited frequent bursts of envy in the soul of the mighty conqueror. Thou," that is, Don Zeltner, " loaded not with rapacious spoils, but bending under the weight of honor, alone hast to fear no such interruption to thy joy, since thou hast already reached the goal to which no hero ever yet attained."

And lest Soleure, in his return, should be wanting in grateful plaudits to this most illustrious

lustrious captain, these Heliconian attornies kindly communicate a spark of their celestial fire, and in bold personification introduce the city herself singing—" O, how art thou come back, invincible son, rich in honors, and adorned with *golden* glory! clemency and justice follow in thy train, and these are the proud trophies which attend thee on thy return. Never did the eastern shores witness so noble a triumph, or Athens, or Sparta, or any other city around, as I who hail this happy day, which gives me back the chief of immortal heroes. Thus," add these Bards of Lugano, " thus thy country sings, unknowing, Illustrious Zeltner, what car of triumph to prepare, or what choice garlands of flowers to weave around thy brow."

SONETO

SONETO I.

I.

Quand Aleſſandro dal domato Eufrate
Al patrio ſuol carico d'or movea
In mezzo ai plauſi de le ſchiere armate,
Da bimo cor meſti ſoſpir traea:

II.

L'oſſa d'Achille nel cammin mirate
Deſtato avieno de la tromba Achea
L'ingrata rimembranza, onde più fiate
Di bell' invidia il fier Campione ardea.

III.

Tu non di ſpoglie ma d'onor ſol carco
Alcun non temi d'affrontar cimento,
Che d'ogni Eroe già ſuperaſti il vanto.

IV.

Quind, il Cereſio dolce empiendo incarco.
D'eletti carmi un vivo monumento,
A tua virtude offre, e conſacra intanto.

SONETO II.

I.

Oh qual ritorni, invitto Figlio a' tuoi
Ricco d'onori, e d'aurea gloria adorno?
Siegue Clemenza, e Aſtrea il tuo ritorno,
E teco porti alti trofei a noi.

II.

Non tal vidder trionfo i Lidi Eoi
Ne Atene, o Sparta, o altra cittade intorno,
Come or ti veggo in ſi felice giorno;
Andar faſtoſa tra i piu degni Eroi.

III.

Coſi la patria dice: e non ſa come
Ne qual, Zeltner, illuſtre, a te prepari,
Cocchio a trionfi tuoi, ſerto alle chiome.

IV.

O d'almi Eroi citta feconda, e chiari,
Onora pur di si gran Figlio il nome;
Figlio, che tanto illuſtra i‑Patri Lari!

What were the diftinguifhed acts of this ex-bailiff, which raifed him in the fongs of his enthufiaftic admirers above Alexander, or what was the triumph he had merited, fuch as Athens or Sparta never witneffed, we were unable to difcover. Zeltner, we underftood from fome of his brother deputies, was a refpectable captain of artillery at Soleure, who, perchance, had never heard of the bones of Achilles, or the Achean trumpet, the imitative blaft of which was now to convey his own name to immortality.

Amidft the croud of Zeltner's virtues, one, however, appeared prominent; the burden of the fong, ftript of its finery, was to celebrate his return from a rich bailiwick with a treafury empty or moderately garnifhed; and as

"The Mufe forbids the virtuous man to die,"

it is to be sincerely hoped that this remarkable instance of self-denial will not only consecrate his own name, but that future bailiffs will imitate this bright model, and immortalize their governments by affording such examples of disinterestedness, as shall encourage the poetical spirit among these tuneful Italians, who, feeling with our immortal bard that

> " One good deed dying tonguelefs
> " Slaughters a thousand waiting upon that,"

will in future build the lofty rhyme to every succeffive bailiff, and be prodigal of praise, in proportion as their governors are sparing of property.

Having yet seen little more than that part of the lake which forms the bay, on which the town is situated, and invited by the beautiful prospect from the terrace of St. Lawrence, we left the noble company at at Lugano, in the full glow of mutual compliment and congratulation, to spend the remainder of the day in sailing along the shores. The lake about half way down divides into two branches, one of which leads to the village of Porto, and the other to the village called Capo di Lago, the Head of the Lake, to which we directed our course. It was the feast of St. Lawrence, and the whole country seemed animated on the occasion. After visiting some of the villages and churches in the neighbourhood, we returned to Capo di Lago, where a repast was prepared for us of fine trout, just fished from the lake by our boatmen, who, guessing that we felt some admiration of grand scenery, had removed our table from the house, and spread it under the shade of a birch tree which hung over the edge of the waters. We had scarcely finished our frugal meal, when distant choral sounds, which came from the adjoining woods that skirted the lake, ftretch upon the ear, and we foon beheld a long line of priefts defcending in their fumptuous robes, preceded by the banners of religion, and followed by a proceffion of well-dreffed villagers of every age and fex, who were chanting refponfes to the facred hymn,

The philofophers are probably right, who declaim againft the fatal interruptions to induftry, from the frequent feftivals in Catholic countries; yet we could not help perceiving, in the groupe before us, an air of fatisfaction and happinefs, which is the great end of toil and labour. Perhaps we were led to lay our philofophy afide, and obferve the homage paid to St. Lawrence, with particular complacency, from the gratification afforded us, by the picturefque appearance of his votaries, winding down the mountain with tapers, banners, and crucifixes, finging the praifes of their patron,

and

and furnifhing a fpectacle far more ftriking to the imagination, than the ufeful employments of the fame clafs of people on the other fide of the Alps, bufied in felling the noble pine, planting hemp-feed, or hoeing tobacco.

The fetting fun beams had fallen upon the lake before we reimbarked, and were reflected in long columns of light upon its limpid waters, which were gently agitated by the foft evening breeze. We had failed in the morning down the right fide of the lake, and now returned to Lugano in the oppofite direction along banks, where the dark rock fometimes rofe abrupt, and bare from the water; but the gay larch that had ftruck root in its crevices, foftened as it floated in the air the gloom of its fhaggy brow: and fometimes the olive, and the fig-tree, though not objects of graceful form

form, contrasted agreeably the wildness of the scene.

In passing before the church of a village, placed at some little distance on the slope rising from the lake, and embosomed among trees, between two steep mountains, we were again saluted with sacred song. It was the Vesperal hymn, proceeding from female voices, flinging its sweet full cadence upon the breeze, and dying along the waters.

Our boatmen slackened their oars, and catching the fond enthusiasm, sung the chorus in tones far from inharmonious, and in which they were joined by passengers of their acquaintance, to whom, with some confidence in our good nature, they had given a place in our boat; while, at intervals, a small company, who were seated on the edge of the water to enjoy the evening frefhnefs, caught and prolonged the notes.

Twilight had fpread all its doubtful fhapes and mild gradations over the fhadowy fcene before we reached Lugano, where we found a numerous affemblage feated on the terrace, opening to the waters, or fipping lemonade in the caffinos: fome were chanting fongs, not in honor of St. Lawrence, but of their miftreffes, and others forming mufical or dancing parties in the adjoining pavilions; fo that the magnificent high and mighty Lords, the Swifs burgeffes, their fovereigns on the other fide of the mountains, could not be more happy, with all their power and glory, than their Italian fubjects of the charming regions around the lake of Lugano.

The town of Lugano is the feat of bufinefs as well as pleafure, being from the navigation

vigation of the lake, the chief entrepot of the commerce carried on between the northern part of Italy, and the countries beyond the Alps. There is alfo a printing eftablifhment in this town, where the proprietor of a Gazette, called The Lugano Journal, has the boldnefs, under the rod of power, to record the political events of the times with truth and impartiality.

Having finifhed our excurfions in the environs of this beautiful country, we returned in a more foutherly direction over Mount Cenere, towards the Lago Maggiore. The view from the fummit of the mountain, over the extenfive lake, ftretching to the Borromean Iflands, and the fertile plains of Lombardy, is highly magnificent. Thofe far-famed iflands, we were obliged, from political confiderations, to leave unvifited, not without a figh of regret on my part, that fince Swifs territory extended fo far beyond

yond its natural boundary the Alps, it had not repelled the limit of the Emperor's dominions a little farther. At the village of Meggedino, lying at the foot of Mount Cenere, we took a boat, and in two hours were conveyed acrofs the lake to Locarno; which town is fituated on its eaftern fide, and forms a picturefque object beneath fteep mountains.

This bailiwick, about fifteen miles in length and breadth, abounding in pafturage, wines, and fruits, was given like Lugano to the Swifs Cantons by the Duke of Milan.

On our landing, finding the ftreets a defert, we ftrayed through the town in fearch of its inhabitants, whom we found affembled in and around a church, preparing themfelves for a folemn fervice, which was to take place the following day. We rambled

bled through the town; parts of which are pleafant, but it wears upon the whole a dull and monaftic appearance. If one may judge from the number of churches, priefts, and convents, compared with the number of houfes and inhabitants, there is no fpot among thefe mountains, where a perfon may efcape fo entirely from the buftle of this world, and find fo many guides to conduct him to another. The inhabitants, we were told, had lately been increafed by a clafs of unfortunate French, whofe profpects were then falling faft into the fhade. We faw a number of them fauntering idly along the walks; and as all evils are relative, it was impoffible to obferve, without fympathy, thofe once gay and gallant nobles, wearing out life in the liftlefs folitude of Locarno.

CHAP.

CHAP XVIII

A Storm on the Lake.—Return to Bellinzone.—Visit to a Convent—Installation of the Bailiff of Bellinzone.

One of the inconveniences of travelling in mountainous countries, is the extreme capriciousness of the weather. Amidst those regions of storm, the unsheltered traveller feels the full blast as it comes fresh from the airy cavern; but no where is its violence so dangerous as on the lakes, which, enclosed between lofty mountains, receive the strong currents of the tempestuous winds in their struggle through the narrow spaces, and suddenly raise their troubled waters into foaming fury. The extreme heat of the weather had long presaged a thunder storm; but although we saw clouds at a remote distance gathering on
the

the summits, we had little apprehension on embarking, that we should feel their discharge before we reached the opposite shore.

Our boatmen, more experienced than ourselves, had warned my companions, as I was afterwards informed that the breeze was on its way, and offered to return the following morning; but among my fellow travellers were three Englishmen, and the newspapers waited for them at Bellinzone. Storms, when weighed against newspapers, were found light in the balance, and the vessel was ordered to be got ready. We had nearly reached the middle of the lake, before the tempest, which we saw gathering thicker on the hills, began to agitate the waters. At first the lightning flashing in white fantastic streaks, and the lofty thunder echoing along the mountains, were objects of pleasing, though awful admiration; and we were

were indulging ourselves with the hope, that the storm was passing away harmless, when a burst of wind struck on the lake, and threw the foaming waters into our bark. It was too late to return, since the wind rushing down the lake, which we were crossing, would have rendered retreat as difficult as going forward.

The storm increased every moment, and the boatmen attempted to make land at any point, but their efforts were ineffectual. Our progress was so slow in the struggle with the waves, that we feared night would overtake us before we could reach the shore; and every person in the boat becoming sensible of the danger, seized the oar, and relieved each other by turns.

After much terror on my part, and much labor on that of my fellow travellers, perhaps mingled with a wish, that they had left Europe to its fate till the next morning, we reached a diſtant part of the ſhore, where, ſheltered from the tempeſt, which continued with unabated fury, we coaſted it back, finding it impracticable to land, and arrived at Maggedino towards the cloſe of the evening. We were ſtill nine or ten miles diſtant from Bellinzone, and were haraſſed and fatigued; but an obſtacle preſented itſelf more inſurmountable than the Gazettes to our remaining in this village, which was the want of every kind of accommodation, either of food or lodging. We recollected alſo, that we were at the foot of Mount Cenere, the haunt of robbers and aſſaſſins; and there was nothing in the looks of thoſe we ſaw around us to inſpire confidence. While we were deliberating what courſe we ſhould purſue, undecided between the danger of remaining in this inſulated ſpot, and the inconveniences we ſhould ſuffer in braving the tempeſt, the ceaſing of of the rain decided us to go on to Bellinzone.

Unacquainted with the road, and afraid to ask a guide of the surly host, we had not proceeded far, when it became so dark, that we could perceive no object, but by the frequent flashes of lightning darting from the livid clouds, while sometimes the menacing roar of torrents, rushing fresh from the hills across our way, was unheard amidst loud bursts of thunder. We were almost in a situation of as much danger as on the lake, since we knew, that before we reached Bellinzone, we had a considerable stream to cross, and feared, that swelled by rains from the hills, it might have become impassable. In this perplexity, a friendly light appeared at a distance, which proceeded from the window of the Cure of an hamlet we were approaching. He invited us to enter, but we put his politeness to no further

further teſt than requeſting his interpoſition with ſome of his pariſhioners for a guide, which he immediately went to a neighbouring hut to procure, and under his auſpices we reached, after midnight, Bellinzone and the journals.

Bellinzone, the joint property of the Cantons of Uri, Schweitz, and Underwalden, was originally, like the other Italian bailiwicks, part of the hereditary poſſeſſions of the Duke of Milan. In the beginning of the fifteenth century the Barons of Miſa, in the Griſons, who had won this territory from the Milaneſe, ſold it to the Cantons of Uri and Underwalden, together with the diſtricts of Bolleny and Riviera, for two thouſand four hundred florins. The Duke of Milan, deſirous of regaining this part of his hereditary dominions, offered to pay the Swiſs the money they had advanced, but feeling that they had made a good bargain with the Barons of Saxe, they were not disposed to treat upon the same terms with the Duke of Milan, who, after much fruitless negociation for the purchase, concluded the affair by seizing on this important key to his states, which he took by surprise. All the Cantons, except Berne, armed to avenge the outrage of thus possessing himself of a town which had been bought and paid for; but after a fierce struggle, the Swiss were obliged to relinquish the contest, and left, in the piles of bones that adorn the chapel of St. Paul, near Bellinzone, the scene of one of their most celebrated battles, a monument, not only of their heroic valour, but perhaps also of their folly, in passing their mountains to mingle in the quarrels of other states After this severe lesson, the Swiss, convinced that no solid advantages could result from the conflict, however gloriously maintained, concluded a peace with the Duke of Milan in 1426, by which they surrendered all their territory on the Italian side of the Alps, on condition of being allowed certain exclusive advantages in their commerce with the Milanese states, and receiving ten times the sum for which they had purchased Bellinzone. In the beginning of the sixteenth century, during the frequent revolutions in Lombardy, the inhabitants revolted, and placed themselves under the protection of the three Cantons; Sforza, Duke of Milan, and Francis the First, gave up their respective claims and the Swifs have ever since retained possession of this bailiwick.

Bellinzone is rich in fine churches dedicated to St. Peter, St. Stephen, St. Blaise, and St. Rock; here are also numerous convents of Augstines, Ursulines, and Recollects, which we visited under the auspices of a very intelligent and amiable emigrant priest. There was little to attract the notice

tice of travellers in thefe calm retreats of ignorance and devotion; though the good monk, who fhewed us the treafures of his convent, fituated beyond the German gate of Bellinzone, intreated we would confider, with attention, a picture hanging on the wall of a chapel, which he affured us was a piece of fingular value, being a true copy of the Virgin, executed by one of the apoftles, and which, having been loft in Turkey, was found ftuck in the walls of a church at Rome, without the aid of any vifible agent to tranfport it thither. He was proceeding with ftedfaft gravity, to give a large detail of the hiftory for our edification, when he underftood, by the blufh which arofe in the countenance of our more fagacious prieft, for the honor of his religion, degraded by fuch fables, that the miracle was breathed into the ear of heretics.

We alfo vifited the convent, or rather fe-minary,

minary, called the Refidence, where we were received with the moft cordial politenefs by the fuperior, a man of erudition, with amiable manners, and a much more agreeable countenance and figure than was neceffary for a monk. In this feminary there are profeffors of the languages, of moral and natural philofophy, and a library, which, confidering the fcarcity of literature in this country, was very refpectable. Young perfons are boarded and educated for about twelve pounds a-year, and the children of the town and neighbourhood receive their education without any expence. This convent has been lately founded, for the building is fcarcely finifhed, with a part of the fuperfluous wealth of the Abbey of Einfilden; and happy would it have been if monaftic wealth and influence had always been employed to fuch ufeful and beneficent purpofes.

The superior, who has the title of prevot, has written a manual of education for the democratic Cantons, of which he presented us with a copy. Admission to the interior of this convent is not allowed to females; and the exception in my favour was a privilege of no little distinction; some of the long galleries, at the end of which we passed, were, however, forbidden ground to a female foot, as I perceived, by the polite observation of the superior, that his jurisdiction extended only to certain parts of the house, one of which was his own private apartment, where we found not only books in great profusion, but hospitable refreshments of every kind.

The administration of this province, like those of Lugano and Locarno, is remitted every two years to a new bailiff. As this event was about to take place, we remained a few days longer, in order to observe whether the Muses

Muses of Bellinzone twined laurels round their bailiff's brow with as lavish profusion as those of Lugano. The morning of this distinguished day was spent in marshalling such of the inhabitants and officers of state as were to go out to meet the new bailiff, and conduct him in procession to his new government. In the evening we beheld the august train, glittering in long gold-laced cloaks, mounted on fiery coursers, and preceded by trumpets, winding along the valley. On their approach within sight of the town, the cannon on the ramparts of the three castles fired alternately a long salute, the roar of which, re-echoing amidst the mountains in a vast variety of successive sounds, was by far the most interesting part of the ceremony.

The next morning, after the celebration of mass, the new bailiff was installed with nearly the same solemnity as at Lugano,

gano, with refpect to form, but with lefs fplendor as to the effect. Few appeared to feel any intereft in the confecration, except thofe who were immediately concerned in the diftribution of the power or the profits of this high dignity, the amount of which laft, we underftood, was inconfiderable, when the compliments were deducted that are paid by the new bailiff to his brother fovereigns on his nomination. Singular anecdotes are'related of the frank and un-difguifed manner in which thefe matters are arranged at the place of election, and which difplay the character of " that fierce democracy" in no very proud point of view.

The knowledge of thofe hiftories is not loft on the people, and it is eafy to perceive that they begin to regard their bailiffs rather as tax-gatherers, legalifed to plunder them, than upright diftributors of juftice, the prefervers of their profperity and peace.

Of the virtues or excellencies of the new governor nothing had yet tranfpired, but we were left in no uncertainty refpecting thofe of the ex-bailiff, Don Francefco Aloifco Wirfch, of the illuftrious Republic of Underwald, and firft captain of the Swifs regiment of Underwald in Spain, in whofe praifes we found the bards of Bellinzone even more fublimely tuneful than the lyrics of Lugano. The poets laureat of Captain Zeltner had only raifed him above Alexander, and made him merely equal to the gods, comparing the triumphs of Soleure to thofe of Athens and Sparta, and thus bounding our imagination to the heroes of Greece and Macedonia; but Captain Wirfch's poet, raifed into more than Virgilian rapture, with " a mafter's hand and prophet's fire," thus ftrikes the immortal ftring:

Exult, break forth in fongs—O, Underwalden,

walden, for thy great son returns to his native shores—what an immortal splendor gracefully plays around him! alike only to himself, " none but himself can be his parallel."—The Holy Virgin descending from heaven, the object of our adoration and worship, takes him by the hand, and bestows on him a profusion of tender caresses. O, Underwalden, after Wirsch, the object of our idolatry, send us another soul of celestial mold, for souls of celestial mold are the prolific produce of thy happy soil.

SONETO.

Esulta esulta; alla tua Patria sponda
Fa ritorno Ondervald il tuo gran Figlio
Quanta luce immortal l' orna, e circondo!
Solo a se stesso, e a null' altro il somiglio.

La Santa Diva, che dal Cielo nacque,
Cui s' ergano gli altari, e i templi anch' ella
Per mano il prese, e lo bacio piu volte.

Deh Ondefvald, dopo *Wirfch*, che tanto piacque
Un altra pur ne manda anima bella
Mille bell' alme hai nel tuo grembo accolte.

Such is the ftyle of panegyric, with which thefe fubtle Italians attempt to foften the native hardnefs of their German bailiffs, and feek to wheedle fucceeding governors into courteous behaviour, by perfuading Mr. Zeltner, that he is equal to the gods, from whom he defcended, and Mr. Wirfch, that he is like no one but himfelf, and the favorite of the Queen of Heaven. Had thefe fonnets proceeded from the pen of fome comic rhymefter, who chofe to amufe himfelf at the expence of bailiffs, we fhould only fmile at the pleafantry; but when we behold the various corporations of thefe provinces, ecclefiaftical and civil, gravely prefenting fuch abject and impious flattery, we fcarcely know whether our indignation is moft excited by the meannefs that degrades

grades itfelf to offer this vile adulation, or the miferable vanity that ftoops to receive it.

The conquered nations of Afia, we are told by the hiftorians, were the firft inventors of this fervile mode of paneygric, and the governors of thofe provinces its firft objects. The Roman proconful, who departed a citizen from the free and equal feat of government, became at once a provincial divinity, with altars and facrifices. We blufh to hear Cicero requefting his brother Quintius to conftruct a temple to his fame, or increafe the number of his ftatues. The fubjects of Lugano footh their conquerors by cheaper arts, the labors of the fong The principle of Swifs government in thefe bailiwicks, is, no doubt, contrary to every inftitution of liberty; yet as in fome religions the conduct of their profeffors is often more humane than their creed, fo in thefe governors,

governors, if we do not find the wifdom and virtue of Cicero, or any other of his qualities, except his vanity, we are at leaft happy in meeting with no imitators of Verres or Geifler.

CHAP.

CHAP. XIX.

History of an Emigrant Family.

OUR excursions, in the neigbourhood of Bellinzone, had more than the charms of new and sublime scenery to imprint them on my memory: a moral interest has impressed them on my heart. There accident led me to the dwelling of Madame C———; and I cannot resist indulging myself by relating the incident, to which I owe the few short, but well-remembered hours, which were gilded by the charm of her society. I will not name the valley, where I found her, and by so doing expose her cottage to the profane gaze of curiosity: but without discovering her abode, I may safely describe its situation; since in that romantic country, how many cottages are placed, like hers, near the steep bank of a torrent stream, surrounded by luxuriant vegetation, veiled by festoons of vines, sheltered above by the hanging woods of fir and pine, and bounded far beyond by the bare rock, and the shining Glacier.

In one of our rambles, at some distance from Bellinzone, we ascended a mountain, the summit of which, we were told, commanded a prospect that would repay us for the toil. The path, however, we found, not merely steep, but so rugged, that before we had ascended half way, we were obliged to alight from our horses, and the evening being too far advanced to admit of our reaching the summit, and returning on foot, we agreed to walk down the mountain, and take a ride along the valley. The gentlemen, who were with me, led their horses, our guide had charge of mine, and I followed them down the narrow shadowy path,

path, sometimes loitering behind to gaze upon the wild and romantic character of the scene around me; sometimes pausing to catch the shifting lights amidst the rude foliage, till I lost sight of my fellow travellers, and soon after reached a spot where two paths met. I could not recollect by which we had mounted, and after some hesitation took the wrong path, hastening my pace, though the descent was difficult, in hopes of rejoining my fellow-travellers. After descending a considerable time without meeting any human figure, or perceiving any human habitation, I reached at length the base of the mountain, where I found some scattered hamlets encircled with vineyards, and entered them in search of a guide. But the cottagers were at their labours in the valley, and these little dwellings were deserted of their inhabitants. The evening was now advancing, and Bellinzone was too distant to be reached on foot till late

late in the night. Nor was the idea of a folitary walk in darknefs agreeable, in a country often infefted by banditti, who find a retreat amidft the wild haunts of Mount Cenere.

About a league from Bellinzone, we had been fhewn the fpot where a traveller was murdered a week before our arrival; and we had feen a picturefque promontory of the lovely Lake of Lugano, deformed by the hideous fpectacle of two men hung in gibbets. The character of the lower order of people, amidft thofe mountains, had appeared to us fomewhat favage; and although I fhould have felt myfelf perfectly fafe under the fhelter of a Swifs cottage, on the other fide of the Alps, I had here no fuch perfuafion of fecurity. After fome deliberation, I determined to wait near the cottages for the return of the labourers; and if my fellow travellers, who were doubtlefs in
search

search of me, did not arrive before that time, to hire an horse and guide to Bellinzone. I sat down on the fragment of a rock, musing on the singularity of my situation, when I heard the approach of footsteps, behind me, and turning my head, saw a lady and gentleman coming along a narrow path, which led to the spot where I was seated. I rose immediately, and advanced towards them, related my adventure, and asked their advice and assistance. The lady, taking my hand with a sweet smile, and a look of benevolence, told me how fortunate she considered herself in being able to render me any service. After making known her name, which denoted high nobility, this emigrant lady, for such she was, intreated me to allow her to conduct me to her cottage, which was within a few paces of the spot where we stood; but persuaded that my fellow travellers were in search of me, I preferred remaining within

within fight of the road, and was anxious to lofe no time in taking meafures for re-turning to Bellinzone.

It was agreed, that a peafant of a neighbouring cottage, whom the lady told me fhe could fafely recommend, fhould procure me an horfe, and convey me to Bellinzone; the gentleman regretting that illnefs put it out of his power to conduct me himfelf; the truth of which affertion his pale countenance and emaciated figure fufficiently evinced. While we were arranging thefe matters, a little rofy-cheeked boy, of three years of age, who had been fporting up and down the mountain-path, as lightly as the playful chamois, came fpringing to his mama, and announced the approach of ftrangers. A few minutes after my fellow travellers, who had re-afcended the mountain a confiderable way in fearch of me, by a different path from that which I had taken,

taken, appeared: the horses were waiting in a little nook, at no great distance, and I hastily took leave of my new acquaintances, but not till the lady, who bade me farewell, with kind reluctance, had made me promise to return with my friends the next morning, to breakfast at her cottage.

During our ride home, and the whole of the evening, I could think and talk of nothing but the charming countenance of Madame de C―――: I tried it by all the rules of Lavater, and was probably a better physiognomist than usual, having so lately heard the subject descanted with a master's art; for it is certain, that on this occasion, my judgment was unerring.

The next morning we set out to breakfast at the cottage: my spirits were exhilarated with the thoughts of visiting my new acquaintance, and I enjoyed more than usually

usually the beauties of the wild romantic valley, along which we rode, and which was gilded with gay sunshine. A torrent stream rolls noisily over its stony bed in the midst of this woody vale, which is rich with pasturage, and bounded on each side by lofty rocks and mountains, while that chain of Glaciers, from which the Rhine pours its source, lift their eternal snows in the distance, and cool the air in the valley.

Fragments of rock were strewed on the edge of our path, and on one spot the vestiges of an avalanche appeared in heaps of massy stones, mingled with the ruins of devastated cottages, and gave a savage wildness to the scene. Soon after crossing a light arched bridge, over-grown with lavish folds of ivy, we reached the mountain, at the foot of which was placed the vine-covered cottage of Madame C———: her sweet little boy stood at the door, watching

for

for our arrival. He danced with delight, while we difmounted; and the moment he could reach me, gracefully kiffed my hand, which is one of the firft things little French boys are taught to do, and then galloped away in fearch of his mama.

The cottage, which was perfectly neat, contained a little plain furniture, two frames filled with ornamental work, a table heaped with drawings, and a fmall fhelf, on which a few books were ranged. Madame de C—— received us with animated pleafure, and her hufband expreffed as much fatisfaction as the languor of ill health feemed to admit. Victoire, a fmart brown girl, whom on a Swifs mountain, or in any other remote region, where I had met her, I fhould immediately have recognized by a gracefully familiar eafe of manner, tempered with the moft profound refpect, for a Parifian *fille de chambre*, prepared the breakfaft fast with a light elastic step, and a look of chearful alacrity.

Madame de C——'s conversation shed flowers over the repast; there was something like enchantment in finding in a rude hamlet, at the foot of savage rocks, and untrodden Glaciers, the most polished graces of intellectual culture; and united with a superior understanding, with a taste for all that is elegant in the arts, and an enthusiasm for all that is sublime in nature, that cordial warmth of manner, that fascinating frankness, when the soul seems to hang upon the lips, and the glowing expression of its sensibility exerts an irresistible influence over the hearts of others. Monf. de C——, an amiable and accomplished man, appeared to be in a state of dejection, which it cost him an effort to conceal, but which his wife was evidently at pains to cheer. After breakfast, Madame C—— proposed a walk

amidst

amidſt ſome of the wildeſt haunts of that romantic region, where ſhe told me ſhe ſeldom met any human creature, and therefore conſidered that portion of the valley as her own territory.

Before we ſet out, Victoire, who ſeemed not a little anxious to know "my opinion of things in general" at Paris, was ſo extremely voluble in her inquiries, that I found it impoſſible for my anſwers to keep any pace with her queſtions. Victoire's mind was fertile in ſuppoſitions, as well as inquiries; ſhe ſuppoſed the monſters had, by this time, ſown all the Tuilleries with potatoes, and dug up the houſes as well as the cellars for ſalt-petre, and made all the women wear red caps; as if it was not bad enough to be forced to ſtick on a cockade, or be dragged to priſon by thoſe horrid *ſans-culottes*, calling themſelves Brutus and Ariſtides. She ſuppoſed too they ſtill went on on with their faucy *tutoiment* and *citoyenne*, to the women—fhe did not know why the brutes dared to call her *citoyenne*, fhe, who had lived all her life at Verfailles, and waited only on court ladies.

Victoire proceeded in her obfervations till I interrupted her by remarking, that fhe muft no doubt find herfelf very happy at fuch a fafe diftance from Paris, among thofe fine mountains.—" Ah, Madame," interrupted Victoire, " happy among the favages here, who can't fpeak one word of French!—Oh, what I would fometimes give for a walk upon the Boulevards! I am fo tired of rocks and fnows!—if it was not for the pleafure of ferving my dear lady, I believe I fhould go back and have my head cut off—for I'm too well known in Paris to efcape—and yet, I muft own the truth, I did all I could to make my lady come away, for certainly, when all
the

the *haute noblesse* were gone, my lady, as I told her, was not made to stay behind— and, indeed," added Victoire, " I was ashamed myself of being seen in Paris, for all the *femmes de chambres* of my acquaintance had emigrated an age before." Upon the whole I observed, from Victoire's conversation, that her wrath and indignation against the Jacobins was almost entirely confined to their *grossiéreté*; as for their cruelty, that seemed to come within the pale of her forgiveness; but to put innocent people to death, and be *mal-honnête, en outre*, she considered as quite unpardonable.

After a delightful ramble amidst the picturesque scenes of that wild country, Madame C—— and myself seated ourselves on a spot of turf, and left the rest of the company to extend their walk. Here, laying aside the tone of general conversation, Madame de de C—— related to me the particulars of her fituation, which fhe probably faw I was anxious to know, more from a fentiment of fympathy, than a principle of curiofity. Nor fhould it be thought fingular that fhe confided her ftory to a ftranger; even an Englifh woman, in that diftant region, furrounded only by half-civilized mountaineers, would have felt confidence fpringing in her bofom towards a perfon who could underftand and pity her feelings; but it required lefs than the folitude of Alpine mountains to have led Madame C—— to unfold her heart. The French are naturally communicative; they neither practice, nor comprehend, that referve which belongs to the Englifh character, and which fometimes has its fource in delicacy, fometimes in pride.

Whatever the French feel or fuffer, hope or fear is readily imparted to the whole circle

cle of their fociety; even perfonal infirmities and mental defects, of which the poffeffor happens to be confcious, are all made known without hefitation; poverty itfelf, which in England we are fo careful to conceal, cofts the French no fuch trouble; nor have they any idea of enduring the fmalleft privation, in order to hide their circumftances or make a better appearance to the world.

But to return to Madame C——, who was the daughter of a nobleman of high rank; and who, at fixteen years of age, had married Monf. C——, by whom fhe was paffionately beloved. That Madame C—— was beloved, I could very eafily believe, while I difcerned the graces of her mind, and beheld the fine expreffion of her countenance, from which forrow; not time, for fhe was now only in her twenty-fourth year, had fnatched the firft frefh tints of beauty,

beauty, but had left an expreffion which blended a more tender fentiment with admiration. Monf. C——, who detefted the principles of the revolution as cordially as moft men of the fame rank, was only prevented from emigrating when firft that event took place, by the reprefentations of his wife, whofe more enlarged mind exulted in that change of fyftem which fhe dared not openly applaud: fhe had often wept over the miferies of the oppreffed people, and was more difpofed to rejoice in the amelioration of folid fubftantial wretchednefs, than to lament the ideal deprivations of greatnefs. After the memorable tenth of Auguft, fhe had no longer power, however, to reftrain her hufband from emigrating, and confidering it as her firft duty to follow his fortunes, and fhare his deftiny, fhe was only prevented from going with him by his defire that fhe fhould endeavour to preferve their property, by remaining in France till the counter-revolution arrived, which he was firmly perfuaded was at no great diftance. After making the tour of Switzerland, he croffed the Alps with a party of emigrants, and finding, that although the counter-revolution was on its way, its march was lefs rapid than he had expected, determined to wait for that event at Bellinzone. Not long after, that ferocious tyranny with its train of horrors, to which regal defpotifm was mild, and all its abufes light, eftablifhed itfelf in France. Madame de C——'s correfpondence became every day more difficult and dangerous, and at length the friend to whom his letters were addreffed declared, that if this epiftolary intercourfe was continued, it would lead not only himfelf, but Madame C——, to the fcaffold.

Deprived of all communication with her hufband, and a melancholy witnefs of crimes which she execrated, and of miseries which she deplored, she soon became herself involved in the general calamity. All the property of Monsf. C—— was sequestered, and the seals were placed upon every apartment of his hotel, after a strict search had been made for Madame C——, who escaped imprisonment by having found a temporary shelter for herself and her little boy, in the house of her friend. This person, a man of sense and virtue, who, abhorrent of the sanguinary measures which then prevailed, had, from circumstances of a private nature, some influence with one high in power, and was ever ready to employ that influence for the purpose of doing good, or rather of averting evil, found means to snatch Madame C—— from danger, by obtaining passports for her and Victoire, as the wives of two Swiss traders, who had come to Paris upon affairs of commerce, and were returning to their own country.

Madame

Madame C——, after thanking her friend for life, since life was then included in the gift of a passport, set off in the diligence to Basil, with her little boy in her arms, and accompanied by Victoire.

During the journey Madame C—— had many alarms on account of the intemperate resentments of her waiting-woman, who, whenever any incident happened by which she was offended, was ready to betray all. Victoire was astonished that nobody found out that she was the *femme de chambre* of the lady of a *cordon rouge*, and was as angry at what she considered as disrespect, to use the words of Johnson, as " the Czar of Muscovy, when he passed through Sweden in disguise." It required many a private lecture, during the route, from Madame C——, to make Victoire preserve the incognita; she longed to burst upon the impertinent fellow-travellers, who greeted her with *tu toi, citoyenne,* and *egalité*, with a detail of all the former splendour of her lady, a large portion of which she considered as reflected upon herself. She owned that she was dying to tell them, that they were not fit company for the anti-chamber, and that this was the first time she herself had ever travelled in a diligence. Madame C—— promised Victoire that she should tell all, and act the duchess if she pleased, when once they had passed the frontier, but conjured her in the mean time, if she valued her life, to be silent; this, however, did not prevent Victoire from declaring to an inn-keeper, who she thought had used too familiar a tone, that she would take care to prevent Monsieur from ever employing his house again; upon which she was heartily abused as the diligence drove off, and met with the usual Jacobin reproof for making use of that appellation, by being told that Monsieur was at Coblentz.

Madame

Madame C——, in spite of the imprudent sallies of her waiting-woman, and some inquiries in the artless accents of her little boy after his papa's coach and four, reached Basil in safety, where she had no sooner taken possession of an apartment at the inn, than Victoire endeavoured to compensate herself for the restraints of the journey, by bawling out her mistress's titles to every waiter in the house, and recounting, with extraordinary volubility, the indignities they had suffered on the road. Poor Victoire, however, met with far less sympathy than she expected, her mistress having, unfortunately for the effect of her harangues, stopped at the Three Kings, which is the resort of the French Republicans, instead of going to the Stork, which is supported by the French Emigrants, and where her tales of plebeian impertinence would have produced a becoming horror.

After one night's repofe, Madame C——having written to announce her arrival to her hufband, and intreat him to meet her at Lucerne, immediately proceeded thither. Two days fhe waited impatiently at Lucerne without any tidings of Monf. C——, and fearing that her letter had mifcarried, determined, without further delay, to crofs the Alps, and joyfully furprize him by her appearance at Bellinzone. As fhe drew near that city her heart fwelled with almoft incontrolable emotion—her hufband had, in fome of his firft letters to her, defcribed the landfcape fo much in detail, that every object feemed to bring his image more vividly to her mind. As fhe paffed over the bridge, about a mile from the town, and faw at a little diftance on the right the Moefa and the Teffino mingling their ftreams together, fhe recollected his having told her, that often on the fpot where their waters met, he leant whole hours

hours in melancholy mufing over their blended currents. She gazed eagerly, as fhe approached the town, at the three frowning caftles that crown the lofty hills, where fucceffively refide the fovereign bailiffs of the fubject valley in which Bellinzone is placed. Monf. C—— had climbed thefe hills, had traced the fcene inclofed between their rocky heights, and ftretching beyond the romantic valley leading to the Italian part of the Grifon territory. Mad. C—— paffed through the gates of Bellinzone, her heart throbbing with thofe overwhelming, thofe delicious fenfations, which are felt when we expect, in a few fhort moments, again to behold the object of our deareft affections, after a feparation embittered by the pangs of calamity, and the apprehenfions of danger. Thofe delightful emotions flufhed her cheek with the glow of animated hope, and bathed her eyes with thofe luxurious tears, which are the attribute of

tender

tender happiness. Madame C——, with her little suite, rode up to the inn, where her husband lived at Bellinzone, and eagerly looked round as she dismounted, in hopes that her letters had by this time arrived, and that the trampling of the horses feet had led him to the door; for her heart told her how wakefully, had he been expected, she would have listened to every sound that could denote his approach, and how quickly she would have sprung to welcome him.

" Where is Monf. C——?" she inquired, with precipitation, not seeing him appear. Monf. C——, the people of the inn informed her, had left their house three months since.—" Where, where is he gone?" exclaimed Madame C——, her heart sickening with disappointment.—He was gone to Constance; but this was not all—he was gone with Madame ——, who

who found Bellinzone too dull for a longer residence. Madame C——, without uttering another word, followed the inn-keeper into the house, but before she had reached the apartment allotted for her fell senseless on the ground: she was carried into her chamber, and laid upon a bed, where, on recovering, she found Victoire anxiously watching at her side. The unfortunate Madame C—— was only restored to a distracting sense of misery; of a species of misery, which her feeling heart was least able to sustain, that of being forsaken by him, whom she loved with the most tender, the most inviolable attachment.

Involved in the consequences of his emigration, she had been forced to bid a final adieu to her country; her country, which she believed would one day shake off the horrible tyranny under which it then groaned, and which she abandoned for ever with regret;

regret; since she felt powerfully that local attachment, which a cold supercilious philosophy may call prejudice, but of which a mind of sensibility is ever strongly susceptible; in consequence of his emigration she had lost all chance of retaining that ample property, which was the splendid inheritance of her child: without sharing the intemperate violence of his political opinions, she had determined to share his misfortunes, and soften that eternal exile to which she flew with reluctance, but which had been his voluntary choice. To be forsaken by him, forsaken at the very moment when mutual confidence, and unshaken fidelity and attachment, were the dear sole refuge left against the storms of fate, was anguish insupportable. How keenly did her breaking heart feel the sentiment, which our divine poet has expressed—

" Had

"Had it pleafed heaven
"To try me with affliction, had he rain'd
"All kinds of fores and fhames on my bare head,
"Steep'd me in poverty to the very lips,
"Given to captivity me and my utmoft hopes,
"I could have found in fome place of my foul
"A drop of patience—
"But there, where I have garner'd up my heart,
"Where either I muft live, or bear no life,
"———— to be difcarded thence!"—

Madame C—— knew too well the character of the lady, who was the companion of her hufband's flight, to doubt of his infidelity. Madame de ——— was a Parifian lady of high rank, who had been diftinguifhed in the ancient regime for the brilliancy of her coteries, and the number of her adorers. Exquifitely fkilled in all thofe meretricious arts, which too often captivate the fenfes of the Lords of Creation, without leave of their reafon, and even in oppofition to all their better feelings, Madame de ——— had for many years enchained

chained in quick fucceffion more captives than fhe could count at her triumphal car; had difturbed the peace of a great number of families; had broken the heart of many a tender female, from whom fhe had alienated the affections of a beloved hufband, by thofe feductions which fpread an alluring drapery over the form of vice, and render the fimple charms of virtuous love infipid to the vitiated fancy. Madame de —— was publicly known to be a woman of galantry, but this by no means prevented her being perfectly well received in the firft circles of fafhion, where fhe was certain to find many who rivaled her in licentious difpofitions, but none who eclipfed her in Circean graces.

Though her youth was now paft, her perfon was ftill attractive, and her gaiety and wit were inexhauftible. The revolution diffolved Madame de ——'s coteries, difperfed dispersed her adorers, transformed Paris into a new region, where the altars of pleasure were overthrown, where incense was offered at the shrine of a new goddess, and where Madame de ―― was stunned from morning till night with the enthusiastic acclamations of the vulgar, whom she had been accustomed to consider as only born for slavery and silence; and who now, lifting up their hoarse voices, for ever thundered in her ear from every quarter the sounds of liberty, and the rights of man.

The morning, after the first Federation, disgusted with that spectacle of happiness, and sickening at the recollection of those shouts of exultation, which arose in unison from half a million of assembled people, Madame de ―― ordered post-horses, and set out for London. Her chief solace in that capital consisted in amusing her former English acquaintances at Paris, by whom

she

she was well received, with spiteful pleasantries upon the new order of things, fanciful definitions of liberty, and ludicrous sketches of the raw parti-coloured volunteers, who, since Madame de —— drew their pictures, have scaled the Alps, and changed the face of Europe.

While that lady was enlivening the various tea-tables where she visited, with well-turned epigrams on democracy, she was summoned by her friends to hasten instantly to France, in order to save her property from confiscation, and herself from being comprized in the law, which placed those persons on the fatal list of emigrants, who did not return within a stated time. Madame de ——, however, with full confidence in her own powers of extricating herself from all scrapes, and overcoming all obstacles, loitered in London till the day of grace was past. She at length came to Paris, and
opened

opened her career in that city, by playfully jesting in society, even with persons in authority, on the subject of her emigration, the events of the revolution, and her own patriotic principles. But the bloody arena of revolutionary government was at that time prepared, the victims were already marked, the horrid forms of death were about to be let loose, and Madame de ———'s *bons-mots*, which were delightful in the safe vicinity of Grosvenor-square, appeared very nearly allied to madness in the neighbourhood of the square of the revolution: as the flowering foliage of the light shrub, which sports gracefully with the perfumed zephyrs in the sheltered valley, assumes a terrific character, when it waves over an Alpine precipice. Madame de ——— finding, that under the fear of the guillotine, people were entirely insensible to wit; and at length being convinced, that all her witcheries and enchantments would be lost upon

upon the fierce demagogues who were about to feize the reins of power, and that fhe was even in fome danger of the fcaffold, fet off for Switzerland with a falfe paffport, accompanied by a young nobleman, who had alfo procured one for the purpofe of joining the army of Condé.

Madame de ⸺ had not fucceeded in faving her property from fequeftration, and her purfe was but lightly furnifhed when fhe left Paris; that of her fellow-traveller, however, was well filled, and Madame de ⸺ was rich in fpells fo potent, that for her

"The royal banner, and all quality,
"Pride, pomp, and circumftance of glorious war,"

were forgotten, till his purfe became as vacant as her own, and fhe then fuffered him to leave her at Bellinzone, and haften to the army with funds fcarcely fufficient to pay the expences of his journey. During this interregnum in Madame de ——'s conquests, Monf. C——, in evil hour, arrived.

He was silent, dejected, and melancholy, which little suited Madame de ——'s taste, but he was in possession of a large sum of money, a circumstance which was not ill adapted to the state of her finances. Madame de —— soon transformed herself into a

> " Pensive nun, devout and pure,
> " Sober, stedfast, and demure."

It was a considerable time before her artillery of wiles made any impression on Monf. C——; her pride became piqued, as well as her interest engaged, in atchieving this new conquest; and Monf. C——, after a siege of considerable length, was added to the number of her captives.

When her dominion was securely established, she insisted upon leaving the solitudes of Bellinzone, of which she had long been heartily weary, for the more congenial region of Constance, which, for dissipation and pleasure, vied with the Paris of former times; and where Monf. de C——'s purse furnished her with all the means of voluptuous luxury.

In the mean time, the unfortunate Madame C——, heedless of the remonstrances of her faithful Victoire, and indifferent to the innocent prattle and sweet caresses of her child, passed some weeks at Bellinzone in that situation of mind, when every care, every affection, and every thought, are absorbed in one deep, powerful, overwhelming sentiment of misery. She was rouzed from this inactive despondency by finding herself menaced with an evil which she had often pitied, but once had little chance of ever

ever feeling; this evil was poverty; not that figurative poverty which pines in artificial want, but the laſt terrible extreme of real miſery; miſery which weighs with its deepeſt preſſure on a mother's heart, when ſhe hears the complaining voice of her child, and has no power to ſupply its neceſſities. Madame C—— had left France with a ſum of money little more than ſufficient to defray the expences of her journey; but ſhe félt no anxiety on this account, as ſhe was going to join her huſband, who ſhe knew was provided, at his departure, with funds which muſt ſtill be more than ſufficient to ſupply all preſent exigencies; and for the future ſhe looked forward to the efforts of their friend in France, to reſcue ſomething from the wreck of their property.

Since her arrival at Bellinzone, ſhe had thought little on the ſubject, for amidſt the first sharp pangs of wounded affection, the lacerated heart, only awake to one sensation, turns with disgust from all the cares, the anxieties, and views of ordinary life; the world seems one wide cheerless desart, and all that it contains, except the object we have lost, has no power to excite an emotion of pain or pleasure.

From this lethargy of despair Madame C—— was awakened, by Victoire telling her that she had heard that the inn at which they lived was extremely expensive. She immediately sent for her bill, though without much alarm, since her repasts had, she thought, been too simple to be costly. The amount of the bill, however, so far exceeded her expectation, that when it was paid, a few remaining livres and a few trinkets were the sole property she possessed. Madame C—— looked at her child, and felt that she had no moments to lose; she determined

termined to leave the inn immediately, and Victoire, after some research, hired a small chamber, containing too wretched beds, to which she retired. Here Madame C——, who had her whole life been nursed in the bosom of affluence, scarcely allowing herself the scanty sustenance which nature requires for its preservation, bathed her child with tears of bitterness, till sometimes the infant caught the infectious sorrow, and wept because he saw her weep. Sometimes he inquired why his mama had no dinner; and sometimes asked why, since he was a good boy, she gave him no *bons-bons* now? Victoire chearfully shared her lady's dry crust, and the only point on which they differed was, that she occasionally gave vent to a sharp reflection on her master, which Madame C—— instantly repressed; upon which Victoire usually left the room, and indulged her feelings, as well as her loquacity, by relating the ſtory, in terms little meaſured, to the whole neighbourhood.

Madame C—— perceived with anguiſh, which can be ill defined, that, notwithſtanding all the privations maternal tenderneſs could deviſe or practiſe, her little funds were almoſt entirely exhauſted; and ſhe had now recourſe to her watch and rings, as the laſt means of averting want from her child. Victoire was forced to part with theſe relicks of former ſplendor at a price far below their value: alas! in ſuch ſort of conventions there is uſually an unequal conflict between rapacity and diſtreſs; but at that period the ſame ſad neceſſity had forced ſo many unfortunate fugitives to relinquiſh, like Madame C——, the appendages of departed opulence, that the quantity of jewels, trinkets, and watches, offered for ſale in Switzerland, had naturally diminiſhed their worth

With

With a trembling hand Madame C——
received the produce of her laſt reſources,
while ſhe anticipated the moment, when
they would altogether fail. The people of
the town, where ſhe had alighted, had before her arrival, diſpatched the letter to
Monſ. C——, which ſhe had ſent him
from Baſil,. but ſhe had received no tidings
of him in return; it was therefore evident,
that he was unaffected by her ſituation, that
he was careleſs of her fate, that he thought
of her no more! Amidſt the bitterneſs of
of thoſe reflections, how eagerly would ſhe
have welcomed that death to which he
abandoned her, but that ſhe muſt leave her
child to periſh. She had not neglected to
inform her friend in France of her circumſtances; but her letter, which it was death
to receive, had to travel by a route ſo circuitous, and to paſs through ſo many hands
before it reached him, that nothing could
be more uncertain than its arrival.

With a frame languid from suffering, and a heart desolate with despair, Madame C—— was one evening sitting in her wretched shed, lost in gloomy meditation, when Victoire, who had been out in search of their little daily supplies, hastily entered the room, and told her, that having been to pay a visit to the people of the inn, where they had lodged, and where she had been talking of her lady's misfortunes, a person who was present said, that if Madame could embroider waistcoats, work cravats, or draw landscapes, she would undertake to sell them to the mistress of the principal inn at Surfee, who made it her business to dispose of such little sort of works, which were executed by some emigrant ladies who lived in that town; and she was sure the same benevolent person would do as much for Madame, when she knew her story.

Victoire

Victoire had proceeded thus far, when Madame C—— threw herself on her knees, and poured forth a fervent thankfgiving: fhe then folded her little boy to her bofom, and inftantly difpatched Victoire to make known how thankfully fhe accepted this bleffed offer. Early the next morning the neceffary materials were purchafed, and Madame C——, with eager alacrity, began her tafk. While fhe contemplated the firft elegant performance, which advanced rapidly beneath her creating hand, tears of foothing pleafure, tears which it was luxury to fhed, gufhed from her eyes. To have the power of applying thofe accomplifhments, which fhe had only cultivated as the amufement of a folitary hour, to the dear, the precious purpofe of fuftaining her child, filled her mind with the fweeteft fenfations of maternal tendernefs—it was delight, elevated by the noble confcioufnefs of duty—it was an effort of virtue, which, while it fhielded the object of her fond solicitude from suffering, was interwoven with an immediate recompense in the soothing effect it produced on her own mind. Since, amidst continual occupation, that gloomy despondency, which in stillness and solitude brooded over its own turbulent wretchedness, was softened into milder sorrow, and engrossed by the unceasing care of providing for her child, the image of its father, which used to call forth the wild agonies of disappointed passion, but now awakened a tender melancholy, which resignation tempered. The only moments which Madame C—— gave to leisure, and the indulgence of her feelings, were those of twilight, when, after the unremitting labours of the long summer day, she usually left her little boy to the care of Victoire, and walking out alone amidst those scenes of solemn grandeur, indulged that mournful musing, when the mind wanders over its vanished pleasures,

and

and tears, which flow without controul, embalm the paſt!

In one of thoſe ſolitary walks, ſeated on the fragment of a rock, near the torrent-ſtream, the hoarſe noiſe of whoſe melancholy waters were congenial to her meditations, the chain of penſive thought was ſuddenly broken by the tread of an approaching footſtep. She caſt up her eyes, and beheld Monſ. C——, who, pale, and trembling with emotion, threw himſelf at her feet, claſped her knees in unutterable agony, and at length told her in broken accents, that he came not to ſolicit her forgiveneſs, but to die in her preſence—that feeling he had but a ſhort time to live, he had ventured to behold her once more, not to attempt any extenuation of his guilt, or to declare how much he abhorred himſelf for the paſt, but merely to explain the appearance of that

barbarous

barbarous neglect, in which she had been left at Bellinzone.

Monſ. C—— then, after execrating the delusion, by which he had been so fatally misled, related, that having taken an excursion into Germany, at the period when her letter arrived, he had only received it two months after it was dated. Rouzed as from an hideous dream, seized with the pangs of remorse at his own conduct, and feeling every sentiment of renewed tenderness awakened in his heart by the image of her sufferings, he instantly declared to Madame —— his resolution to hasten to Bellinzone. No intelligence, he perceived, could be more agreeable to that lady, and not long after he discovered the reason, by hearing that she was gone to Vienna with a German Count, the owner of a brilliant equipage, with whom she became acquainted during

during their excursion, and who had followed her to Constance. Monf. C—— added, that having himself set out on foot from that city, being determined not to spend on the indulgence of a carriage the few louis he had yet in reserve, the violent emotions of his mind, joined to excessive fatigue of body, by taking journeys too rapid, in order to accelerate his arrival, produced a dangerous fever. At a little village-inn, where he lay for several weeks stretched upon a solitary bed of sickness, he had perhaps, he said, in some measure atoned for the past, by the bitterness of his regrets, by that anguish—he was proceeding, when Madame C—— threw herself upon his neck, bathed his bosom with her tears, conjured him for ever to forget the past, and declared, that her sufferings had already vanished in the hope of his returning affection.

When

When Madame C——, with soft persuasion, had somewhat reconciled her husband to himself, and a calm confidential conversation had succeeded the tumultuous emotions of their first meeting, they bent their way to the little apartment which was now their sole habitation, and which he had not yet entered; since having learned from the people of the house, in Victoire's absence, which path Madame C—— had taken for her evening walk, he had instantly hastened to the spot. They had scarcely reached the chamber, when his little boy sprung forward to meet him, clung upon his neck, called him his dear, dear papa, and reiterated his caresses till Monf. C——, overcome with faintness, agitation, and fatigue, sunk senseless on a chair. Madame C—— wept at observing his emaciated figure, and his pale and haggard look; and Victoire, she perceived, tried to squeeze out a tear too, but not succeeding, all she could do do was to wipe her eyes carefully with her handkerchief. Victoire was probably thinking more of the dry crufts on which fhe had dined occafionally, and which fort of repafts fhe attributed to her mafter's conduct, than of his fickly countenance. Madame C—— found nothing more difficult than to reftrain Victoire's loquacity, who contrived, whenever fhe had an opportunity in the courfe of the evening, to relate the hardfhips they had fuffered with a fpiteful minutenefs of detail—how Madame breakfafted upon cold water inftead of coffee, and dined fometimes upon lentil-foup, and fometimes not at all; and how fhe gained two livres a-day by drawing and embroidery.

This laft intelligence was more than Monf. C—— could bear; he hid his face with his hands, fprung from his chair and walked in a difordered manner up and down

down the room. Madame angrily impofed
filence on Victoire, who, taking the hint,
declared that fhe was *au defefpoir* at having
afflicted Monfieur, for whom fhe felt the
moft profound refpect, and then left the
room, in order, probably, to talk over his
tranfgreffions to the whole neighbourhood.
She ftaid fo long, that Madame C—— was
forced to go in fearch of her, and as fhe
approached, heard her faying, " to be fure
I don't forget that Monfieur is a *cordon
rouge* after all, and therefore not made to
give an account of his actions to any body;
but then when I think of my dear lady"—
here Victoire was interrupted in her unfinifhed fpeech.

Monfieur had a return of his fever,
which lafted fome weeks; and, at
length, believing he had fuffered fufficient penance, Victoire gracioufly accorded him her forgivenefs. A fhort time
after

after, the return of Monf. C——, a letter arrived from their friend in France, with tidings that he had fecured for Madame C—— a fum fufficient to produce a little revenue, which would place her out of the reach of want, and which fum was depofited in the hands of a Swifs banker. Upon receiving this intelligence, they determined to leave their wretched apartment, and having, in their rambles along the wild valley leading to the Grifons, difcovered a neat vacant cottage, they hired it for the fummer; there Monf. C—— hoped to recover his health amidft the falubrious breezes from the hills, and his peace of mind amidft the calm and foothing fenfations which the fimple beauties of unadorned nature can beft excite.

After repeated vifits to her charming cottage, I bade Madame C—— a long, reluctant farewell; and have fince heard, with

with delight, that fhe continues in the privacy of her retreat to enjoy that domeftic blifs, which, to fenfibility like hers, is the firft of bleffings; fhe has a mind capable of relinquifhing rank and fplendor without a figh, fince fhe has found happinefs in exchange.

CHAP.

CHAP. XX.

Visit to the Grisons.—Discussion on the Revolution.

IN one of our rides near Bellinzone, we made an excursion along a valley belonging to the Grisons. Fatigued with the beams of the noon day sun, we looked around for the inn of the village, and accepted the invitation of a person, of whom we made the inquiry, and over whose door we saw an inscription that denoted the asylum, of which we were in search. The hour of dinner was past in the valley, but a plentiful collation of fruits, wine, and cakes, were set before us. On our entrance we found three or four persons in warm political debate; but the principal disputants were a gentleman of Turin, who had lately passed some time at Paris, and a young ecclesiastic

clesiastic belonging to an adjoining village. As the subject of dispute was the revolution which had just then taken place in the Grisons, we were led to ask for information respecting it.

The native of Turin informed us, that that event was nothing but the transitory commotion of an ignorant and tumultuous mob, that on some idle pretence had assembled together to correct abuses that did not exist, had seized on the government of the country, committed great depredations on the property of individuals, and were on the point of being reduced to their primitive nothingness, as the good sense of the country revolted against proceedings so destructive of peace and order. The ecclesiastic listened with considerable impatience to the end of the harangue, when, with an eloquent volubility, that proved how earnestly his heart was engaged in the cause, he he ran over the long lift of tyrannies exercifed on the people by the Ariftocratic governments, which had juft been overthrown. He attefted that this tumultuous rabble was a regular affembly of the reprefentatives of the people deputed from each commune, and who had met as a legal convention to reform in the moft conftitutional manner thofe abufes. He affured us, that fo far from committing depredations on property, perhaps the only blame to be caft on the convention, was the lenity with which they had treated thofe offences, which had neceffitated the change of government, fince all they had done was to order a repayment into the public treafury from each defaulter of the unaccounted monies; but this was exacted in fuch fmall proportions, that the fentence feemed rather an invitation to offence than a punifhment for paft depredations.

The reforms in the future adminiftration, he afferted, were not lefs mild than the lenity exercifed againft the abufes of the paft. The people were relieved from the burden of taxes that were never applied by their former governors to the fervice of the ftate, and the feudal rights of the nobility were abolifhed; that with the exception of the flight retributions made to the public purfe, and the lofs of certain privileges, by more equality in the regulations of commerce, the nobles had nothing to lament, but a degree of influence, which they ought never to have poffeffed, and were even permitted to retain all the infignia of their ancient dominion, all the decorations of family and title. So far, continued our ecclefiaftic, was this affembly of the people from being reduced to what was called primitive nothingnefs, that having only before them certain fimple objects of reform, in which they were unanimous, they had adjourned their

their meeting, merely becaufe they had finifhed their work; and fo far were they from having acted contrary to the wifh of their conftituents, that he believed, except from thofe who were immediately interefted in the continuance of ancient abufes, there was but one voice throughout the whole country, that of enthufiafm for the recovery of their rights, which, if again attacked, all were ready to defend, or perifh in the attempt *.

The reply of the Piedmontefe to his an-

* It appears that this young ecclefiaftic had formed too favourable an opinion of his new governors on the other fide of the mountain; and it is probable, that he and the other inhabitants of the Valley of Mifox have fince changed their manner of thinking: fince it is faid, that the people of this valley, now the only part of the Grifon dominions on the fouthern fide of the Alps, have folicited their junction to the Cifalpine republic; between which two countries are fituated the Italian bailiwicks.

tagonist was witty and sarcastic; but it was
easy to perceive, by the triumph painted in
the countenances of the by-standers, that
the priest had echoed their own sentiments.
Our inn-keeper joined in the conversation,
with an authority equal to his guests; but
though deeply interested in the debate, was
careful to go at certain intervals with a
spoonful of lemonade to wet the parched
lips of a feverish infant, who lay in its
cradle in a corner of the room. Its sister, a
girl of six years of age, drest in a blue boddice, and short red petticoat, with her feet
and legs bare, and whose cheek flushed with
the clearest bloom of health, and eye spark-
ing with sprightliness, formed a striking
contrast to the languid look of the pale
baby, stood patiently at the side of its
cradle, with a large vine-branch in her
hand, which she waved backwards and for-
wards to prevent the numerous flies, that
noon brings forth in that country, from

teizing

teizing the fick child. There was something fo attractive in this domeftic groupe, that they often made me forget the Grifon revolution.

Two hours had glided away before we thought of ordering our horfes, when we received a moft cordial invitation from a venerable old man of the party, to pafs a few days at his dwelling, in our paffage over his mountains, having heard that we propofed returning through the Grifon country.

We were not a little embarraffed at the miftake we had made, when upon inquiring what expence we had incurred, our hoft replied, that the only recompenfe he defired was our fpeedy return at an earlier hour to dinner: when we fhould be received, not as he faw we fuppofed ourfelves at an inn, but at the habitation of a friend, a friend, who would be thankful for the favour. Our inn-keeper proved, on inquiry, to be the principal magiſtrate of the diſtrict, and the inſcription, which we had taken for a ſign, was an ornament over the door of his houſe.

CHAP.

CHAP. XXI.

Val Calenca State of Society.—Journey up St. Bernardin.—Lavanges.—Grifon Hospitality.—Pastoral Occupations.

WE did not fail, on leaving the Italian vallies, to pass two days with our hospitable host, the greater part of which were spent in excursions amongst the mountains, particularly those of the Val Calenca, which is one of the four districts of this jurisdiction, called the high jurisdiction of the Valley of Misox. A rapid torrent flowing from the Glaciers of the Bird Mountain, runs noisily through the Valley of Valenca, and throws itself into the Moesa. We passed through several villages, but stopped to repose ourselves at Santa Maria, the capital of the Valley, where we saw a magnificent church

church dedicated to the Virgin. The laſt village in this diſtrict, or the neareſt to the Glaciers, is Val Bella, or the Beautiful Valley; but as we were aſſured that the place did not at all correſpond with the name, we diſcontinued our journey thither. This valley, ſituated between the mountains of Val Bienna and thoſe of the Valley of Mifox, is extenſive, but for the moſt part wild and barren; it is not eaſy to find a place in the world ſo little known to it, as this ſecluded and ſavage nook. The ungrateful ſoil prompts the inhabitants to periodical emigrations; the ſummer is ſpent in the native hut, and the winter is the ſeaſon of travel and obſervation, the expences of which are defrayed by the produce of their manufactures, ſuch as baſkets, pitch, grinding-ſtones, and other territorial mountainous productions, which they ſell in Italy. Thoſe who are not engaged in commercial projects, and the wives and children of thoſe

those who are, follow other speculations of profit, among which are those of begging and predicting the *buona aventura*, or telling fortunes.

After taking leave of our kind host, we proceeded on our journey along the Valley of Misox towards the Bernardin mountains. This valley is one of the four high jurisdictions below the woods, into which the Grison league is divided. The ancient inhabitants are known in history under the general term of the Lepontii, but their descendants were successively subject to the Bishop of Como, the Counts of Saxe, and the family of the Trivulci. In the middle of the sixteenth century, the inhabitants purchased their freedom of this family for twenty-five thousand florins, and joined themselves to the Grison league, who have maintained the confederacy, notwithstanding the various attempts which have been since

since made to deprive them of their liberty.

The road, for several miles, is perfectly level along the Moesa, and the valley sufficiently extensive to admit of fine cultivation, contains a number of handsome villages; but after passing the confluence of this stream with the torrent of Calenca, the valley becomes so narrow as to admit little more space between the mountains than for the path and the river. Here we were once more among rocks, torrents, and cliffs loaded with woods, presenting not only parts of the mountain scenery, to which we were now accustomed, but from the great depth of the valley closed in by surrounding mountains, casting a kind of gloomy light over the wild landscape, that strongly excited in the mind that sensation of melancholy which Pope has characterised,

"Breathing a browner horror o'er the woods."

Before

Before we came to the end of this lower valley, where the mountain, direct in front, lofty and abrupt, seemed to preclude all possibility of proceeding, we passed for a considerable way over a road entirely broken up, and which displayed the roots of larches, pines, and other mountain trees, mingled with vast mounds of gravelly stones and masses of rock. This desolation had been caused by a deluge from the upper mountains, on the sudden melting of the snows in the spring from an incessant rain, which lasted several days, accompanied by gusts of warm winds, like the Sirocco of Italy. The openings into the ravines of the mountains where the snow had drifted, and from its mass had resisted the influence of the heat which melted the thinner layers, served as sluice-gates to the sea of waters which they ingulphed. The increasing weight of those waters from the melting of the snows above, together with the

the decrease in the resisting mass beneath, from the heat and the rain, prepared at length the cataftrophe, by the giving way of the icy barrier.

Language can but feebly paint the sublime and terrific effects of this deluge of the mountainous sea. Had our poet, Thomson, beheld this mighty devaftation, his glowing imagination would have presented us with far other images than those of

" Herds and flocks, and travellers and swains,
" And sometimes whole brigades of marching troops,
" Or hamlets sleeping in the dread of night;"

the feeble works of human art and industry hurled beneath the smothering ruins. He would have viewed the lofty pine, the ancient inhabitant of the Alps, whose roots have been riveted for ages to the soil, swept away, by the horrible flood, like the chaff; the rocks, coeval with time, and which seemed

seemed fixed on the solid globe till time shall be no longer, torn from their base with irresistible fury, and rolled, in one wild convulsive commotion, down the tremendous precipices, riving up the affrighted soil, in their descent, and covering the fertile pasturage and rich champain with irreparable desolation.

A narrow pass cut out of a fantastic rock, hanging over the Moesa, which forms a bay in the plain, brought us to the foot of this perpendicular mountain, down whose dark wooded and shaggy precipices we heard the torrent roaring, but which their projecting sides concealed from our view. We appeared to be inclosed between inaccessible heights; there was no passage discoverable like that of the cavern which leads from the devil's bridge into the Valley of Urseren, and it would have exercised the imagination, to have built even an ideal road

by which the afcent could be gained. The
mountaineers, however, had overcome the
difficulty; on that fide of the mountain
which was the moft floping, or rather the
leaft perpendicular, a road was cut in tra-
verfe directions to the end of the flope,
whence it was returned in an angle, fufficiently broad to permit the afcent of cattle,
and fo continued from one fide to the other
fupported by beams of wood, either for the
prefervation of the way, or to keep the traveller from ftumbling over the precipice,
till after laborious climbing it brings him
to the fummit.

Like the paffage into the Valley of Urferen, the plain on the top of this mountain prefented us with fcenes altogether different from thofe which we had left beneath.
It is generally in the lower valleys, which
ferve as canals or outlets to the mountains,
that we find thofe romantic and picturefque
objects,

objects, on which we gaze with delight and aftonifhment. In the upper mountains, nature has caft off the fantaftic and varied garb of rock, and cliff, and torrent, for a robe more fimple and majeftic; the fcene takes a larger fweep, the foreft is more extenfive, and the hills fwell with a more noble grace one above the other.

So few are the travellers who pafs this mountain, the principal paffages acrofs the Alps being thofe of St. Gothard and Splugen, that the vifit of ftrangers is an event of fome importance. On our approach to a village embofomed in trees, forming the middle point of an amphitheatre of a beautiful range of hills, covered with the frefheft verdure, we difcovered our venerable friend walking haftily towards us, with a pretty little mountain nymph, his grand-daughter, in one hand, and a large oaken ftaff in the other, which he fhook at us with a fmile of reproach, declaring that he had waited dinner three hours beyond his ufual time, having had news of us early in the morning, and that he could not imagine why we had loitered fo long on the way. We found a plentiful repaft prepared for us, confifting of beafts and birds of the foreft, and were informed that we fhould not be fuffered to depart till the provifion was expended, which the hunting of the two preceding days had furnifhed.

The old man's family confifted of a daughter and her two children, the one a youth of twenty, and the other the pretty little mountaineer of fixteen years of age, who had come with her grandfather to meet us; his fon-in-law, who was then gone on fome affairs to Chiavenna, was expected home before our departure. We fpent the remainder of the day in walking among thefe romantic and paftoral fcenes, and the next

next we made a family party up the mountain, to dine in one of his fhepherd's huts, by the fide of a fine cafcade, which, having found out my enthufiafm for fuch objects, he told me he was fure I fhould find worth the toil of the vifit. The torrent formed part of a beautiful landfcape, and played in fucceffive cataracts over rocks that were picturefque; but we had feen too much of the Reufs and the Teffino, to find in thefe falling waters any new charm, except that they were inclofed by green banks inftead of fhaggy rocks.

Thefe hills appeared, from their verdure, to be in the higheft ftate of mountainous cultivation. The fpot was not fo elevated as to be out of the reach of the parching funbeam, and little channels cut along the fide of the flopes, drew the water away from the idle torrent to fertilize the adjoining paftures. On the greater part of thefe hills

the hay had already been cut. Some yet lay on the ground, which, from the mountain flowers and herbs, scented the air with the most delicious fragrance. While these hills are laid up for harvest, the shepherd removes to the Upper Alps, ascending with his cattle to crop the herbage of those higher hills, as they are successively deprived of their snows. Here he spends a solitary and cheerless life through the short summer, and returns in the autumn to the huts in the lower vallies, where he remains shut up with his cattle to consume the provision which he has prepared for winter. The life of the shepherd of the Alps is very different from that of the shepherd of Arcadia; but from the little intercourse which he holds with any society whatever, except the beasts which he feeds, his wants are only those of nature, and consequently few: the intemperance of the season finds him prepared to meet it without
shrinking

shrinking, and the winter storm flies harmless over his head, whose physical feelings are hardened to the icy temperature of his mountains, and who is accustomed to

" Breast the keen air, and carol as he goes."

Sometimes indeed the patience of the shepherd expires before the winter, when he perceives, which sometimes happens, that his stock decays faster than the summer approaches.

These pasturages are not sufficiently steep for avalanches, but higher up the mountain, partial mischiefs are occasioned by their descent; and sometimes shepherds, huts, and cattle, are lost for a while under immense drifts of snow, which the impetuous winds have sent in that direction. It was difficult for us, the inhabitants of the lower world, to conceive that the change of seasons could make so barren and cheerless a desart of so beautiful and fertile a country, as that which we beheld, seated at our rural repast before the shepherd's door; around which the cattle were browzing, or lay basking in the noon-tide sun-beam. That the summer might be passed agreeably amidst these mountains, we could easily believe; for surely there are few spots on the globe, that can boast a more boundless store

" Of charms, which nature to her vot'ry yields;
" The warbling woodland, and the torrent's roar,
" The pomp of groves, and garniture of fields;
" All that the genial ray of morning gilds,
" And all that echoes to the song of even;
" All that the mountain's shelt'ring bosom shields,
" And all the dread magnificence of heaven;"

But the winter must indeed be gloomily desolate to those, who, above the class of the peasant, and having no taste for literature, are immured in these insulated regions, which

which at that feafon become altogether impaffable.

My pretty little companion anfwered my queftions, refpecting her winter occupations, by telling me, that fhe had returned from fchool at Bellinzone the fummer before, and had employed the laft winter in fpinning and making her grandfather a large quantity of fhirts, had worked a flowered gown for herfelf, and read half of an abridgment of Guicciardini's Hiftory of the Wars of Italy, and two or three volumes of Goldoni's Plays.

We bade adieu, with reluctance, to our patriarchal hoft: I could have loitered with pleafure yet a little longer in his hofpitable dwelling. How foothing was this fcene of tranquil pleafure—how delightful a tranfition from the crimes of ferocious tyranny were the paftoral occupations

tions and guiltlefs manners of thofe Alpine regions! At a village, a few miles further up the mountain, where the whole family conducted us, we paffed one more focial hour at breakfaft, and then finally taking leave of them, impreffed with the moft agreeable recollection of their fimple kindnefs, we began to climb the ftupendous fummits of their mountains, the haunts of eternal winter.

CHAP.

CHAP. XXII.

St. Bernardin.—Misery of the Shepherd's Life.—Emigrant Priest. — Summit of St. Bernardin. — First View of the Rhine.

THE Alps, which we traversed in our ascent, wear, with little variation, the same smiling aspect as in the regions below. When the mountaineers speak of the Alps, they do not mean those long chains of icy or barren mountains, to which we give that appellation, and which, in our language, implies height. In the mountain dialect that term conveys the idea of fertility; and when the inhabitants talk of the Alps, they always mean spots of mountain pasturage. The *Gletscher*, the *Horn*, the *Stork*, are denominations, by which they distinguish different parts of these mountains, and

and the terms of rocky or ice-covered Alps, would to them be unintelligible.

Having climbed to the village of St. Bernardin, and finding ourselves within the influence of the Glaciers, which we saw stretching far before us, we concluded, that we had nearly reached the summit, but learnt that we had yet a league of very rough ascent to pass over before we should begin to descend on the other side. We made a halt at the village of St. Bernardin, if two or three houses, one of which is an inn, and a little building, dignified by the name of a chapel, can be called a village. The country around wears a cheerless, solitary aspect. We were not got beyond the reach of vegetation; but it was a vegetation that made the barrenness of the soil more visible. The inhabitant of the Lower Alps shares no property in this sterile region: the wandering shepherd of the plains alone
steals

steals the winged days of summer, to lead over an unappropriated soil his ragged and ill-favoured flock. His miserable hut is composed of pieces of rock, through the crannies of which the wind and the rain pour without resistance. His chief and almost unvaried food is oatmeal and water; for the soil would reward no cultivation: bread is the produce only of climates far below; he is bereaved even of the most common enjoyments of social life.

In these regions, however, we found one inhabitant of polished manners, and lettered accomplishments. A banished vicar general of one of the principal dioceses of France was dragging on existence amidst these inhospitable climes, barred from all communication with the world during the long winter, and supported by the miserable endowment of the chapel, amounting to six or seven louis a year, and the coarse charity of of the rude mountaineers, who were his sole associates. He told us, that his breviary, his bible, and his Ovid, were his only solace; that from the one he endeavoured to teach himself resignation to the will of heaven, and from the other to sooth his mind, by sympathizing with an exiled fellow sufferer, who, banished from the delights of a court to the deserts of Scythia, could scarcely have found them more dreary than the summit of St. Bernardin. Here also he might have exclaimed with the poet:

" Forced from my native seats, and sacred home,
" Friendless, alone, through Scythian wilds to roam;
" With trembling knees o'er unknown hills I go,
" Stiff with blue ice and heap'd with drifted snow;
" Pale suns there strike their feeble rays in vain,
" Which faintly glance against the marble plain."

Mrs. BARBAULD.

He had been vaguely informed of the fall of Robespierre, and the return of a milder system; and he inquired with such solicitude if there was no hope of his being permitted to revisit his country, that it would have been cruel to rob his sorrows of that fond illusion. We left this unfortunate stranger with sincere regret, that we had no power to extricate him from a situation which seemed almost insupportable.

We now began to scale the remainder of the mountain, and though we felt the icy breeze from the neighbouring Glaciers, we escaped any disagreeable sensations of cold by the frequent exercise of walking, the road being often too steep or too dangerous to continue on horseback. We also enjoyed the rays of a cloudless sun, more brilliant, indeed, than genial, from the extreme rarefaction of the atmosphere at this elevation. We had been told at Bellinzone that the mountain, for two leagues, is always covered with a confiderable quantity of fnow, but without having paffed any, we attained the fummit.

The top of St. Bernardin affords nothing that is ftriking, except its defolate uniformity; here are no maffes of enormous rock, no tremendous precipices, no yawning chafms; no object picturefque or aweful. The ftorms of ages have not only ftript it of the means of vegetation, by wafhing away every veftige of foil, but have humbled the rocks, if any once ftood prominent, to a modeft level with the wafte. The mountain ftill rifing on the right, conceals the Glaciers that feparate the Grifons from the Valteline, but on the left the eye wanders far over thofe regions of eternal froft, which are formed by the eaftern extremity of that chain of mountains, known to the antients under the name of the Adula.

In

In the front the view extends acrofs the valley of the Rhine, to the Glaciers that feparate it from the other vallies of the Grifons. We feemed within reach of thofe Glaciers which we beheld falling, like an immenfe veil, down the mountain below our prefent elevation, and were eager to tread their gloffy furface; but were told that a paffage acrofs from St. Bernardin was impracticable.

After repofing ourfelves on the fummit, amidft this chaos of unvivified nature, we began to defcend on the northern fide. The mountains we had juft fcaled were fo abruptly thrown back, that we could difcern no farther in a direct line before us, than the hill which we were immediately afcending, and often believed we had attained the fummit before we had conquered half the road. On the other fide we were prefented with a majeftic fweep down the mountain, and along the lofty hills that inclose the valley of the Rhine, ſtretching away to the piny foreſts riſing above the Vale of Splugen. After deſcending a conſiderable way almoſt perpendicularly, but on a firm and well-conſtructed road, we came in view of that celebrated river which we had lately beheld bearing its thundering maſs of waters to the ocean, but which, now juſt ſpringing from its ſource, ſteals placidly along the quiet valley, ſoft as the firſt ſleep of infancy after it has waked to new exiſtence.

END OF VOL. I.

For EU product safety concerns, contact us at Calle de José Abascal, 56–1°, 28003 Madrid, Spain or eugpsr@cambridge.org.

www.ingramcontent.com/pod-product-compliance
Ingram Content Group UK Ltd.
Pitfield, Milton Keynes, MK11 3LW, UK
UKHW010852060825
461487UK00012B/1063